SERVICE EVANGELISM

SERVICE EVANGELISM

by
Richard Stoll Armstrong

THE WESTMINSTER PRESS
Philadelphia

Scripture quotations from the Revised Standard Version of the Bible are copyrighted 1946, 1952, © 1971, 1973 by the Division of Christian Education of the National Council of the Churches of Christ in the U.S.A., and are used by permission.

BOOK DESIGN BY DOROTHY ALDEN SMITH

First edition

Published by The Westminster Press®

Philadelphia, Pennsylvania

PRINTED IN THE UNITED STATES OF AMERICA
9 8 7 6 5 4 3 2 1

Library of Congress Cataloging in Publication Data

Armstrong, Richard Stoll, 1924–
    Service evangelism.

    1. Evangelistic work.   2. Witness bearing
(Christianity)   I. Title.
BV3790.A73   254'.6   78-26701
ISBN 0-664-24252-9

Contents

PREFACE   9

FOREWORD   11

1. HOW IT BEGAN   13

    I. The Cry for Help   *14*
    II. The Call to a Church   *15*
    III. The Birth of a Model   *17*

2. THE CASE FOR FAITH-SHARING   21

    I. The Nature and Role of Proof   *21*
    II. The Nature and Role of Faith   *22*
        A. The Basis for Faith   *23*
        B. The Nature of Faith   *24*
        C. The Paradox of Faith   *26*
        D. The Leap of Faith   *29*
    III. Sharing Faith   *31*
        A. Bridging the Gap   *31*
        B. Answering the Why?   *32*
        C. Justifying the Approach   *33*
    IV. Conclusion   *37*

3. A SERVANT CHURCH   38

    I. The Suffering Servant   *38*
    II. Our Chief End   *39*
    III. A Twofold Mission   *40*

IV. A Threefold Function *42*
V. On This Rock *45*
VI. A Commission *46*
VII. An Endorsement *48*
VIII. A Promise *49*

4. SERVICE EVANGELISM   51

I. The Word Itself and How We Use It *54*
II. Evangelism and Witnessing *55*
III. Evangelism and the Evangelical *56*
IV. Evangelism and Communication *57*
V. Evangelism and Social Action *58*
VI. Evangelism and Proselytizing *63*
VII. Evangelism, Christian Nurture, and Church Renewal *65*

5. AN EVANGELISTIC STYLE   70

I. Ambassadors for Christ *71*
II. Always in Triumph *74*
III. The Aroma of Christ *75*
IV. Not Peddlers *76*

6. INTERPERSONAL WITNESSING   79

I. Visitation Evangelism *79*
II. SERVICE Evangelism *81*
III. Service EVANGELISM *82*
IV. The Approach *83*
V. Inside the Home *85*
VI. Some Thoughts About Listening *90*
VII. Some Thoughts About Speaking *95*
VIII. Some Thoughts About Using the Bible *98*

IX. Some Thoughts About
     Witnessing *104*

7. ROLE-PLAYING   114

    I. The Training Task *114*
    II. The Facts Game *115*
    III. An Exercise in Faith-Sharing *117*
    IV. Discovering Role-Playing *118*
    V. The Role of the Leader *119*
    VI. Role-Playing and P.R.O.O.F. *120*
            A. Structuring *122*
            B. Suggestions for Leaders
               125

8. CONDUCTING A P.R.O.O.F. SEMINAR   128

    I. Preliminaries *128*
            A. Recruiting the Participants
               128
            B. Scheduling the Seminar
               129
            C. Setting Up the Room *130*
            D. Preparing for Small-Group
               Activities *130*
            E. Providing for Food and
               Other Essentials *132*
            F. Greeting the Arrivers *133*
    II. Outline for the Seminar Leader *133*
            Thursday Night *133*
            Friday Night *136*
            Saturday *139*
    III. The Evaluation Process *145*

9. PREPARING THE CONGREGATION   149

    I. Sharing the Dream *149*
    II. Establishing the Ground Rules *150*
    III. Planning the Preaching *155*

IV. Identifying the P.R.O.O.F.
Prospects *158*
V. Developing the Support System
159

10. AFTER P.R.O.O.F., WHAT?   162

I. The Calling Program   *162*
    A. Scheduling   *163*
    B. Ambassador Groups   *164*
    C. The Format   *165*
    D. The "Afterglow"   *170*
    E. On-the-Job Training   *172*
    F. Record-Keeping   *173*
    G. Following Through   *175*
II. The Pudding of
the P.R.O.O.F.   *176*
    A. The Callers   *176*
    B. The Church   *176*
    C. The Community   *178*
III. Refresher Courses   *180*

POSTSCRIPT   181

APPENDIXES   183

A. Receiving New Members   *183*
B. Outline of P.R.O.O.F. Seminar
186
C. P.R.O.O.F. Seminar Bench Mark
188
D. P.R.O.O.F.   Seminar   Evaluation
Sheet   *189*
E-1. Ambassador Card   *190*
E-2. Calling Results   *190*
F. The Ministry of the Church-in-Com-
munity   *191*

SUGGESTIONS FOR FURTHER READING   197

Preface

For a long time I have wanted to put into writing some thoughts about a style of evangelism that does not fit the stereotyped images many people have of evangelistic programs in churches. To distinguish what we were doing in the Oak Lane Presbyterian Church of Philadelphia in the late 1950's and early 1960's from some of the other approaches then in vogue, I called it "service evangelism."

Through the years I have developed a rationale for the principles that I had discovered through experience to be true. Service evangelism is based on a particular understanding of faith that I have presented to pastors' seminars at considerable length and depth. In a briefer form, I have incorporated these theoretical foundations into the training model described in the chapters that follow; for I have wanted this "how to" book to be both theoretically valid and practically helpful not only to pastors but also to lay people on struggling evangelism committees in local churches.

I am indebted to the many persons who have, knowingly or unknowingly, been part of the process of developing and interpreting service evangelism, including hundreds of seminar participants with whom I have explored the meaning of faith and members of the faculties of Princeton Theological Seminary and Christian Theological Seminary. In particular I wish to thank President James I. McCord, Dean Arthur M. Adams, and Dr. Jack Cooper of Princeton Seminary for giving me many opportunities to expose my ideas to pastors and others attending the Institute of Theology and various seminars at the Center of Continuing Education.

I also want to express my gratitude to Dr. George E. Sweazey for his excellent critique of parts of the original manuscript; to Dr. Elmer G. Homrighausen for his helpful suggestions and willingness to write the Foreword; to Lynne Morgan, without whose super secretarial skills the publication deadline could never have been met; and to my wife, Margie, proofreader *par excellence,* without whose patience and encouragement the book would never have been written.

Finally, I want to pay special tribute to the Oak Lane Monday Night Callers and the faithful Ambassadors for Christ of Second Presbyterian Church, Indianapolis, whose application of the principles of service evangelism has done more than anything else to prove its value. It is in grateful appreciation to them that this book is dedicated.

RICHARD STOLL ARMSTRONG

Foreword

Evangelism is still a controversial term and a hesitant ministry in many churches. The loss of church membership in some of the largest denominations is a matter of concern. But of even greater concern is the lack of clear motivation, meaning, and methodology in fulfilling the Great Commission to make disciples of Jesus Christ and mature them in the Christian way of life. Evangelism is a must if the church is to fulfill its mission, and yet evangelism is a problem.

Evangelism seems to be the "in" thing in our time. There are scores of "evangelists" appealing for converts to their gospels. They are witnessing through leaders and spirited communities to a generation that is questing for peace of mind, identity, immediate and "high" experiences with the Ultimate.

The religious press is booming because it is fed by a popular demand for stories of those who have "found it," for prescriptions that will produce the highest human potential, for innovative ways by which confused pilgrims will find their identity and a sense of life direction.

And churches and ministers and lay people are deeply concerned about these matters. Today they are wrestling with the church's mission and priorities of which evangelism is a major aspect. Not satisfied with the older style of evangelism that centered largely in personal salvation or statistical growth, nor with the newer interpretation of evangelism that centers largely in social justice or humanization, they are reaching for that comprehensive evangelism which embraces the fullness of the gospel: personal discipleship with Jesus Christ and communal love and relationship with the neighbor.

In the face of the situation in the churches and in culture, it is an encouraging and refreshing experience to read Richard Armstrong's exciting book on evangelism. The reader soon detects that this is not a theoretical theological treatise on evangelism, nor is it a series of surefire gimmicks to increase church membership.

Indeed, this story deals with the theology, the meaning, and the administration of evangelism, but it sets them within the context of a working congregation of Christian people in a real community. The reader constantly senses the relation of the theology and the practice of evangelism. Through it all there is evident the reality of a strong pastoral leadership. This story has been in action for a number of years. During that time Dr. Armstrong has been testing and revising his "service evangelism." And he has presented it in seminars, conferences, and congregations in different situations and areas of the country.

This "program," if it may be so called, confirms our conviction that the best evangelism is done by pastors and people in local congregations, and that where pastoral leadership has the vision and the ability and the willingness to work at evangelism theologically, personally, congregationally, and communally, something creative will happen in the life and work of the church.

ELMER G. HOMRIGHAUSEN

Princeton, New Jersey

1

How It Began

Is the Great Commission out of date?

I think not. We are still called to be Christ's witnesses in the world today. For that reason evangelism is not an option. It is an imperative, and we had better be about the task. The question is, What kind of evangelism?

While serving as pastor of the Oak Lane Presbyterian Church of Philadelphia, I was involved for ten years in a continuous program of visitation evangelism. The results of our outreach led to numerous requests from churches and groups of churches for help in organizing similar programs. They were interested in the "nuts and bolts," but I became increasingly aware of the need to state the Biblical/theological rationale for the particular style of evangelism in which we were engaged. That need in turn led me into an intensive study of the nature, meaning, and role of faith, an interest that continued when I left the pastorate to join the administrative staff of Princeton Theological Seminary.

Two years after leaving Philadelphia I was asked by the Division of Evangelism of The United Presbyterian Church U.S.A. to write a case history of the Oak Lane Church. I agreed to write *The Oak Lane Story* in the hope that others might be encouraged to engage in a similar program, which I sincerely believed then and still believe would benefit any church. I call it *service evangelism.*

I. THE CRY FOR HELP

In the meantime I was becoming more and more involved in an extracurricular ministry, conducting workshops and seminars throughout the United States. There
was a growing demand from many ministers and lay leaders for a theologically acceptable approach to evangelism,
vis-à-vis some of the more conservative and aggressively
individualistic methods being used. Wherever I went, the
same questions were being asked, the same cries for help
were being raised, the same concerns were being expressed:

"What is the real purpose of evangelism?"
"How do you reach the unchurched?"
"Is there any relation between evangelism and social
    action?"
"How do you create a climate of acceptance in your
    church for evangelism?"
"How do you motivate people to want to share their
    faith?"
"Does our religious language really communicate in
    today's world?"
"Will visitation evangelism work in a rural community?
    in the city? in a high-rise development? in a racially
    changing neighborhood?"
"Shouldn't we start with our own backsliders first?"
"What is the pastor's role in all this?"

These were the kinds of questions I kept hearing from
pastors and lay people alike. They seemed to find answers
in a style of evangelism that was service-oriented. Having
an institutional base from which to operate and with the
sanction and support of the seminary, in what was becoming an impossibly busy schedule, I became correspond-
ingly less interested in returning to the parish ministry, as
I had expected to do in time. Such a move would have

meant my having to terminate a teaching ministry that I felt was helping to meet an urgent need.

II. THE CALL TO A CHURCH

But God had other plans. After six years I found myself "back in the saddle" again, as pastor of the Second Presbyterian Church of Indianapolis, Indiana. My new pastorate seemed an ideal experimental training ground for the development of a service evangelism training model, because of the challenges that both the congregation and the community presented. In conducting evangelism seminars I had frequently encountered resistance to the idea of any kind of visitation evangelism program from those who felt that "this kind of door-to-door solicitation simply won't work in a community like ours." A "community like ours" was any community where it was assumed that the residents would be unresponsive to any sort of door-to-door calling. This assumption was most frequently heard from churches in the more affluent communities, whose residents are supposed to be "too sophisticated for that sort of thing." Second Church is in "that sort of neighborhood," with expensive homes and people who enjoy and can afford to protect their privacy. The immediate parish area is fairly stable, though the population is becoming increasingly more transient, as more corporate management personnel, with greater job mobility, move into the area. The community is largely residential. The nearest shopping centers and professional buildings are more than a mile away. The population is predominantly white, with a much higher than average median family income. There are several large Protestant churches, a Roman Catholic church, and two large Jewish synagogues nearby. Four years ago it remained to be seen what the response of our neighbors would be to any outreach from our congregation.

In analyzing the geographical distribution of the membership and those recently joining the church, as well as of the visitors to the Sunday morning worship services, the Long Range Planning Committee discovered that Second Presbyterian Church is more than just a neighborhood church. It is, in their words, a "cathedral" church, which draws from the entire metropolitan area. Its members are spread throughout a wide circle of greater Indianapolis. The committee concluded that the church must try to serve both roles, limiting its evangelistic outreach to those within its more narrowly defined parish area, and yet serving the broader community through the involvement of its members in various worthy activities and causes, and through its financial support.

Although the congregation had a commendable history of mission giving, there did not appear to be any recent inclination toward or even interest in evangelism. There was certainly no mandate from the congregation for an evangelistic outreach. Experience has taught me that deepening the congregation's spiritual commitment is the best way to encourage interest in evangelism. What was needed, therefore, was a training program that would begin by helping people to discover and understand their personal faith in God, before teaching them how to share their faith with others.

That there was a need for a visitation evangelism program in the community remained to be seen, although I knew from experience we would find that at least half of the people in our community were either unchurched or only nominally related to a church. I had found that to be true all over the country, even in the so-called Bible Belt. Whenever I asked the question, "What percentage of the population of your community do not attend any church or synagogue?" the answer was never less than fifty percent. The answers were usually based on the results of a religious census of some kind. I was sure that the situation would be no different in Indianapolis, even though people were saying, "Just about everybody in this neighborhood belongs to a church." My suspicions have been proved to be correct.

III. THE BIRTH OF A MODEL

Before any program could be launched, some groundwork had to be laid. There were many one-on-one conversations, small-group discussions, and sermons from the pulpit. All pointed toward developing an understanding of the concept of service evangelism, and preparing the way for the training program that I eventually called P.R.O.O.F. (*P*robing *R*esponsibly *O*ur *O*wn *F*aith). Suffice it to say that Second Presbyterian Church provided an excellent proving ground for P.R.O.O.F.!

But I wanted the program to be adaptable for use as a training model for other churches as well. That would necessitate the preparation of written materials for distribution to the participants, as well as a publishable version for use as a "textbook" for pastors wanting to use the program in their own churches. For me that meant further theological research and reflection on the meaning of faith, as well as an extensive survey of various evangelistic materials and the study of numerous books and articles on evangelism.

The P.R.O.O.F. model represents the culmination of many years of theoretical study and practical experience. It is, as far as I know, a unique approach. It is only *one* method, not *the* method. Its purpose is to offer what I believe is a viable alternative to some of the popular, but in the opinion of some pastors questionable, evangelistic methods in use today.

The need for such a program was based on my strong conviction, born of experience, that too many church members are turned off by the word "evangelism" and that too many pastors don't know how to turn them on. Not many people feel that they can share their faith effectively. They simply don't know how.

Believing that an evangelistic training model should begin with an exploration of the nature of faith and a shared experience of the reality of faith, I worked up a rough outline for a fifteen-hour seminar, for which I had hit upon the acronym title P.R.O.O.F. The fifteen persons who responded to my invitation to attend the first seminar were intrigued by the idea of an in-depth probe of their own faith, and by the outline which they received with my letter confirming their reservation for the seminar. Aside from the outline and some sheets of Biblical references I had very few materials to distribute at that first seminar.

It was a good experience, and so were the next two, for each of which I tried to put into writing some additional thoughts for distribution to the participants at appropriate points throughout the seminar. Having been invited to conduct a seminar at the Center of Continuing Education at Princeton Theological Seminary in March 1976, I decided to try out the P.R.O.O.F. model at that time. More than fifty ministers had signed up for the seminar, which had been publicized under the title "A New Look at Evangelism." I was encouraged by their enthusiastic response.

Since then I have been conducting periodic P.R.O.O.F. seminars for members of Second Presbyterian Church. Each seminar has provided further opportunity for refining and improving the format and content of the model.

In the twelve-month period between September 1976 and September 1977 three important events transpired which were invaluable in refining the P.R.O.O.F. model. The first was the Midwest Evangelism Conference, co-sponsored by the Synod of the Covenant and the Synod of Lincoln Trails. The conference afforded me an opportunity to present some of the principles of P.R.O.O.F. to several hundred Presbyterians from a five-state area.

The second event had a much more direct bearing on the development of the P.R.O.O.F. model. I had accepted an invitation to conduct an evangelism conference two months later for a group of Presbyterian pastors and lay

leaders from Washington, Oregon, and California. The
conference was held in Corvallis, Oregon, and I took that
opportunity to lead them through the entire P.R.O.O.F.
experience. The response was overwhelmingly positive,
although I was frustrated by the continual goings and com-
ings of those who lived close enough to commute. Experience has shown that one requirement for attending a
P.R.O.O.F. seminar must be a commitment to attend from
start to finish. Our own church members have been unanimous in their feeling that missing any part seriously de-
tracts from the overall effect. The practical application
depends upon one's understanding of the theoretical content, and the theoretical content becomes clear only
through the practical application. Everything builds on all
that has preceded it. The evaluation sheets of some of the
"irregulars" at the Oregon seminar indicated that they
had not really grasped the basic concepts.

The third significant event was the workshop which I
conducted at the Princeton Institute of Theology the very
next month. From this learning experience, I concluded
that for larger groups I would have to develop a different
format, one that would introduce the concepts of
P.R.O.O.F. but would not attempt to give an actual experience of a P.R.O.O.F. seminar. With small groups of pastors
it is possible to do both, that is, show them how to use the
model even as they experience it themselves.

One other important lesson that I learned from the experience at the Institute of Theology, as well as from the
conference at Oregon, was the urgent need for a written
resource. The various materials I had developed were
helpful to the persons who attended the conference, but
they had no meaning for anyone else. They had to be
interpreted in the context of the P.R.O.O.F. experience.
I knew I had to produce a written presentation of the
philosophy and methodology of the P.R.O.O.F. model.

In the meantime I found nothing in my theological research that caused me to doubt the validity of the concept.

On the contrary, the more I read, the more convinced I became that the approach was Biblically, theologically, and experientially sound. But it requires a certain understanding of the nature of faith, which understanding has tremendous implications not only for evangelism but for preaching, teaching, and every other dimension of ministry. For that reason it is essential to talk about faith before we talk about evangelism. We must first make the case for faith-sharing.

2

The Case for Faith-Sharing

I. THE NATURE AND ROLE OF PROOF

The case for faith-sharing begins with an assumption. It is impossible to establish a rational proof for the existence of God that is logically compelling for anyone who does not already believe in God. Yet the very fact that we live in a skeptical world imposes upon us who believe the necessity of substantiating our faith in God.

Unbelievers are constantly demanding that we prove our truth claims. They have a right to examine our arguments before "buying" them, and we should respect their desire for persuasive evidence. That desire is itself a reason for hope, for it shows that those who ask for proof are still open to the possibility of believing.

We need to understand, however, the nature of the proof we hope to offer. It requires hearing as well as speaking; in other words, a two-way communication in which both sides are intellectually honest and open to truth.

If proof is understood to be the irrefutable conclusion drawn from a set of expressed facts, we are doomed to failure from the start. But if proof is the substantiation of a hypothesis by logical argument and supportive evidence, it is possible to "prove" an assumption of faith to the satisfaction of one who holds that assumption.

The task of proof, however, is not just to buoy up the

21

faith of believers, but is to provide an intellectual rationale by which some unbelievers can be convinced. Is there a way to say why we believe in God that will convince an honest doubter who wants to know our reasons? Assuming that a person is willing to listen, what can we say that will convince that person to opt for God?

There has always been and there always will be a need for capable defenders of the faith—neo-apologists—who offer not glib answers, as Job's friends did, but who know what they believe and why they believe it, and who can articulate and communicate that to others in a persuasive and winsome way. The task of the evangelist is not primarily to argue a case but to state one's beliefs in such a way as to enable others to perceive them to be true.

Every theological or philosophical structure has its own presuppositions, its faith assumptions upon which its case for God ultimately depends. Theological integrity demands that those who would convince others of the existence of God should begin by identifying, conceptualizing, articulating, and confessing their own faith assumptions.

The same holds true for those who deny God's existence. They have their assumptions, too. Like those whose arguments for the existence of God they reject, nonbelievers also reason from premises that are ultimately unverifiable.

The ground of all proof for or against the existence of God, therefore, is an assumption of faith or nonfaith, for which evidence must be adduced by the "prover."

II. THE NATURE AND ROLE OF FAITH

With the advent of the linguistic analysis school, however, the question was no longer whether or not God's existence can be proved, but whether or not it is possible to say anything meaningful about God at all. The denial of the validity of God language has serious implications for the proclamation of the gospel and the entire evangelistic enterprise. How does one do evangelism in a pluralistic, materialistic, humanistic, secularistic, "scientistic" society like ours?

A. The Basis for Faith

I began wrestling with this question many years ago, for it was one I had to answer in order to be able to preach with integrity, let alone train people to "do the work of an evangelist." My quest has been a spiritual pilgrimage as well as a theological exercise, as I waded through the German liberal theologians to see how they dealt with the problems of faith and reason, revelation and history, and the subjective-objective dichotomy. What I was searching for was not a proof of the existence of God but a rational basis for my own faith. Proof for me became a dialogue between belief and doubt. I knew that I believed in God, but did I know why?

Whenever I asked others this question, they would respond with their own unsophisticated version of one of the traditional proofs ("When I gaze at the stars in the heavens, I know there has to be a God!"), or from their own experience of answered prayer ("If it hadn't been for God, I wouldn't be alive today"). They were telling, in effect, not why but *what* they believed, and their tautological reasons could never be logically compelling for a nonbeliever.

The more I read and thought about it, the more I realized that one cannot answer the *why* of faith without using faith statements. Our reasons for believing in God must ultimately involve us in a tautology of some kind. To every reason given, one may legitimately ask "Why?" The believer finally arrives at the bottom line, at which point faith's answer to the ultimate *why* is God. But that is an assumption of faith, which is not at all self-evident to the nonbeliever.

B. The Nature of Faith

I have been using faith in what Clark Williamson, in his book *God Is Never Absent* (Bethany Press, 1977), calls the passive sense (having faith), rather than in the dynamic sense of being faithful (faith as a verb). Both uses are legitimate, in my opinion. While it is certainly wrong to equate being faithful with belief, it is not wrong to speak of having faith, where faith is trust as well as belief in God.

The New Testament use of the word "faith" is different from the Greek philosophical use, which primarily meant "trust," in the sense of believing something that could not be proved. Sometimes the Greek New Testament word *pistis*, usually translated "faith," is used simply to signify the Christian religion (Acts 6:7; Gal. 1:23; Phil. 1:25; etc.), with the corresponding Greek verb meaning loyal adherence to it. But the primary usage stems from the Old Testament, where the Hebrew root *'āman* indicates belief in the sense of holding on to something with firmness and conviction. In the New Testament, *pistis* is generally used in the active sense, denoting trust, confidence, conviction. It is rarely used in the passive sense to mean the virtue of fidelity (Titus 2:10; Matt. 23:23). Sometimes it is used in antithesis to sight ("we walk by faith, not by sight," II Cor. 5:7), but the primary antithesis is between faith and works of the law.

Faith is an important word with Paul, who uses it chiefly in connection with Christ. It is trust directed toward Christ. "I know whom I have believed" (II Tim. 1:12). It is not merely giving one's intellectual assent to certain propositions but it is a relationship to God which is grounded in the historical fact of Christ. Christian faith is based on the witness of the apostles about Christ.

The revelation of God and the message of redemption are laden with eternal, transhistorical reality and meaning, which are grasped only by faith. The meaning of Christ's death on the cross can be understood only if we ourselves are identified through faith with that death. Thus our relationship to Christ is grounded in faith ("the righteousness of God is revealed through faith for faith," Rom. 1:17). In short, the faith that Paul talks about is total subjection to and concentration on Christ.

Richard R. Niebuhr is correct in pointing out that faith is not a thing in itself. It cannot profitably be understood as an abstraction but only as it appears in human beings seeking to understand, struggling to be faithful, daring to believe in spite of doubt, hoping, fearing, desiring, trusting.

Niebuhr examines the concept of faith as a virtue of reasoning and as an exercise of willing, and then suggests a third (and better) way. He describes faith as an elemental form of experience, that which was once called religious affection, and which lies at such a depth of personal existence that it is inaccessible to volition.

We are talking, then, about a level of knowledge or experience that is preconscious and prereflective and affects our attitudes and behavior regardless of our conscious beliefs. The latter are important but not all-controlling.

The expression "to have faith" suggests to me a conscious awareness of that preconscious affection. It is a prereflective disposition to believe. Alfred North Whitehead would have said that our prereflective experience is ineradicable, but our conscious beliefs are certainly not. In that sense, therefore, faith as a noun can be the object of a verb, including the verb "to have" and the verb "to lose."

The issue of the relative adequacy of the two expressions, having faith and being faithful, may be only semantic. It seems that their use depends upon what the user intends to say. When Clark Williamson states that faith is an act, he means being faithful. Faith in that sense becomes the living out of one's faith claim. But faith can also refer to the cognitive content of that truth claim, or to one's conscious desire to trust, love, and obey, as well as to believe in God. It is in the latter sense that I have been using the term, and what I was struggling to establish was a rational case for my own faith. Where did my faith come from?—which question is another way of asking, Why do I believe in God?

C. The Paradox of Faith

As I searched the New Testament for Biblical insights I became increasingly aware of the paradoxical nature of faith. Many of the passages relating explicitly or implicitly to my question seem to emphasize my responsibility to believe, to have faith; as when Jesus rebukes the disciples for their little faith (Matt. 8:26; 14:31; 16:8; 17:20; Mark 16:14; Luke 24:25; etc.) or compliments the centurion (Matt. 8:10) and the Canaanite woman (Matt. 15:28) for their great faith. Every time he exhorts someone to have faith (Matt. 21:21) or to believe (Mark 5:36; Luke 8:50; John 6:35, 40; 14:1, 11; etc.), the implication is that the responsibility to believe is entirely ours. So, too, his call to follow him (Matt. 4:19; 8:22; Mark 2:14; 8:34; 10:21; Luke 5:27; 9:23; 18:22; John 1:43), or to seek (Matt. 6:33), or to ask (Matt. 7:7), implies our capacity to believe, and hence our responsibility.

This aspect of faith is evident throughout the New Testament, including the letters of Paul (Rom. 1:16–17; 3:22; 10:9, 14; I Cor. 15:14, 17; Gal. 3:22; Col. 2:5; I Tim. 1:16; etc.). One of the classic expressions is Heb. 11:6: "Without faith it is impossible to please him. For whoever would draw near to God must believe that he exists and that he rewards those who seek him." Other examples are Acts 15:7; 16:31; I Peter 1:7–9; I John 3:23; and the entire eleventh chapter of Hebrews. In all of these passages faith appears as our struggle to believe, man's grasping for God.

An equally impressive array of passages, on the other hand, refers to faith directly or indirectly as a gift of God. For example:

And no one knows the Father except the Son and any one to whom the Son chooses to reveal him. (Matt. 11:27; cf. Luke 10:22)

To you it has been given to know the secrets of the kingdom of heaven, but to them it has not been given. (Matt. 13:11; cf. Mark 4:11)

No one can come to me unless the Father who sent me draws him. (John 6:44, 65)

And as many as were ordained to eternal life believed. (Acts 13:48)

Each according to the measure of faith which God has assigned him. (Rom. 12:3)

The unspiritual man does not receive the gifts of the Spirit of God, for they are folly to him, and he is not able to understand them because they are spiritually discerned. (I Cor. 2:14)

If then you received it, why do you boast as if it were not a gift? (I Cor. 4:7)

And no one can say "Jesus is Lord" except by the Holy Spirit. (I Cor. 12:3)

To one is given through the Spirit the utterance of wisdom, . . . to another faith by the same Spirit. (I Cor. 12:8–9)

Working together with him, then, we entreat you not to accept the grace of God in vain. (II Cor. 6:1)

For by grace you have been saved through faith; and this is not your own doing, it is the gift of God. (Eph. 2:8)

But grace was given to each of us according to the measure of Christ's gift. (Eph. 4:7)

Through him you have confidence in God, who raised him from the dead and gave him glory, so that your faith and hope are in God. (I Peter 1:21)

My experience confirms what the Scripture affirms about the gift of faith. I know that I cannot make myself

believe in God. I cannot conjure up faith. My wife, Margie,
and I discovered this about ourselves when our son Ricky
was dying of leukemia. We were not active church members at the time and certainly not mature Christians. I had
never studied the Bible, nor had I ever attended Sunday
school as a boy, although I had been confirmed in the
Episcopal church at the age of eleven. Margie had grown
up in the Presbyterian church, but neither one of us was
prepared for the terrible shock of learning that our little
boy had a fatal disease.

As we searched for answers to the agonizing Why? we
appreciated the comfort and support of our friends who
shared that struggle with us. One couple, who were Christian Scientists, spent an evening interpreting to us their
concept of faith healing. The message they communicated
to us was that if only we could have enough faith, Ricky
would live. But Ricky died. What a horrible burden it
would have been for us all these years to think that his
death was due to our lack of faith. What comfort can there
possibly be in the thought that my life or that of anyone
else depends on my capacity to believe? Faith is not something I can make myself have; it is something I find myself
with. Faith is not a possession. We don't own it. We receive
it, as a gift from God.

Yet my experience also confirms that faith has been a
struggle for me. It has been my grasping for God, as well
as God's reaching out to me. That's the paradox of the gift
and the grasp. We never know faith is a gift, until we
receive it. When the light of faith dawns, we discover that
God was waiting for us in the darkness of our unbelief.
One of my favorite hymns puts it well:

> I sought the Lord, and afterward I knew
>   He moved my soul to seek Him, seeking me;
> It was not I that found, O Saviour true;
>   No, I was found of Thee.

There will always be that tension between our struggle and God's gift, between the grasp and the gift. When the gift and the grasp become one, then we have faith. But we have it as a gift of God, not as a human achievement. It is the gift of God's grace, not the product of our effort. It is God's revelation, not our discovery.

What we are dealing with, therefore, is not a genuine paradox, but a pseudo paradox, if the ultimate source of faith is God. Words such as belief, desire, response, and trust seem to put the burden of faith on us. But belief implies the capacity to believe, and that's a gift of God. Desire assumes desire-ability, and responsibility assumes response-ability. In other words, the grasp assumes the gift, for the motivation to grasp is itself a gift!

D. The Leap of Faith

Søren Kierkegaard and others who talk about the "leap of faith" seem to be emphasizing our responsibility (the grasp), until we ask whence comes the desire to leap. Before one takes the leap, there is that initial urge, that impulse to leap, and that is a gift of God. Yet we have the freedom to leap or not to leap.

The relationship of the leap of faith to the paradox of the gift and the grasp can be roughly illustrated by a diagram (p. 30) in which two cliffs, one designated "Belief" and the other "Disbelief," are separated by a great gulf.

A, standing on the belief side of the gap, knows that God is there, and for A the wonders of the universe (teleological argument) represented by the stars above, are "proof" of A's belief. A wonders why B, standing in disbelief on the other side of the gap, cannot acknowledge God's presence on the basis of the evidence which is also available to B, who can also look up and see the stars, but for whom the stars do not constitute proof of God. In order for B to view the stars as proof of God, B would have to be standing

where A is standing. It is futile to try to "prove" God to someone standing on the cliff of disbelief.

How does B get from the cliff of disbelief to the cliff of belief? It requires a leap of faith, which expression suggests the possibility that God may *not* be there! That possibility not only does exist, it must exist, for faith to be faith. If B knew that God was there, then B would not be standing on the cliff of disbelief. Perhaps we should call it the leap of hope, rather than the leap of faith. The leap would normally be seen as "grasp"—B's effort to get to God. It is my contention, however, that the *urge* to leap is itself a gift of God. That is to say, it takes some faith to make the leap of faith! That is another way of stating the paradox of the gift and the grasp.

Francis Schaeffer, in his book *The God Who Is There* (London: Hodder & Stoughton, 1968) and in other writings, denies the validity of the leap of faith concept, which he sees as an irrational leap "upstairs." "God is there," he would argue, "and it is therefore meaningless to talk about God as if he is not there!" This is the commonly accepted view of rational conservatism. I contend that if anyone denies the leap, it is only because he has already made the leap! Schaeffer can say that God is there because he is standing on the belief side of the gap. Only one who has taken the leap of faith can say that God is there. The decisions of faith are not made in total darkness but are made according to the glimmers of light one already has.

Thus there is no way to predate God's initiative. The gift always precedes the grasp (resolution of the paradox), but while we are grasping, we are unaware of the givenness of faith. We keep on struggling to believe, and when we finally do, we realize that our struggle was indeed our delayed response to what God had been offering us all along. When we can finally say "I believe!" we know that God was there before we believed. And it is a never-ending process.

III. SHARING FAITH

A. Bridging the Gap

If people are the instruments God uses to reach other people, what can A do to help B take the leap? A can begin by trying to remove any barriers that are blocking B's view of God. Some barriers may be on A's side of the gap, such as the language barrier, by which many Christians lock out others who cannot play their language game. Other barriers may be on B's side of the gap, such as mistaken concepts of God, the church, or Jesus Christ, which ideas, if true, would be reason enough for anyone not to believe in God!

A should go over to B and talk with B *where B is,* crossing over rather than shouting across the gap! A's purpose is to identify with B, to stand where B stands, to feel what B feels. A goes to listen rather than to unload. A's aim is to relate to B and to show B that A cares. By caring, A also hopes to show that A believes in a God who cares, and by being there, A hopes that B will come to understand that God is there!

It is important that A try to understand the nature of B's disbelief. B will respond more readily if A can help B to realize that there are stones of doubt on the cliff of belief as well as on the cliff of disbelief. Faith implies doubt, for without doubt, faith is no longer faith, but rather factual knowledge, that which can be validated by empirical evidence. The opposite of faith is not doubt but separation from God.

Instead of trying to convince B by argument, therefore, A waits for the appropriate moment to share A's own experience, admitting that the evidence is conclusive only to those who already believe. In other words, A must begin by confessing A's own faith assumptions, and A tries to help B identify and articulate B's assumptions, for B has assumptions also. A must understand and help B to understand that even the *desire* to believe is a gift of God. You can't get up earlier than God!

Both A and B must understand, furthermore, that faith is the gift of *God,* not of A. It is God who is the converter, working in A and B to will and to do his good pleasure. It is not A working in B, but God working in and through them both. Thus A's testimony becomes a *confession* of faith, which leaves the focus, the responsibility, and the ultimate credit for revelation to God alone.

B. Answering the Why?

If, then, faith is ultimately a gift of God, can we "share" it? The question has tremendous implications for the way we do evangelism. If it all depends on God, what is our role in the evangelistic process? If it is impossible to say why we believe in God without using faith statements, which are always tautological and ultimately subjective, how do we answer the *why* question?

Having recognized the nature of our reasons, we can then say something like this: I believe in God because I wake up believing in God; or, I believe in God because the God I believe in has given me the faith to say I believe in him; or, I believe in God because I recognize that I want to. These are all tautological statements. I confess that at the outset. They are not provable, not compelling, and certainly not normative. Now I know what it means to "confess" my faith. I am confessing my inability to make myself believe, or to make anyone else believe. I confess that my statements are not a proof but a conviction for which I give the God I believe in the credit. Proof, then, is the confirmation of my belief. All I can do is point to the evidence that confirms my faith assumptions—my experience of answered prayers, my sense of God's presence in my life, the feeling that my needs have been satisfied, the spiritual insights I have received, the testimonies of others who have had spiritual experiences, the historical witness of the church, the authority of the Bible, and so on.

C. Justifying the Approach

That is what I mean by "faith-sharing." I believe it is a Biblically, theologically, philosophically, psychologically, and experientially sound approach. It is certainly a Biblical imperative, as we are commanded by Jesus himself to make disciples of all nations (Matt. 28:19), and to be his witnesses to the ends of the earth (Acts 1:8). Paul reminds us that we are ambassadors for Christ, having been entrusted by God with the message of reconciliation, and he urges those who are taught the word to "share all good things with him who teaches" (Gal. 6:6). "I pray," wrote Paul to Philemon, "that the sharing of your faith may promote the knowledge of all the good that is ours in Christ" (Philemon 6). Peter cautions, "Always be prepared to make a defense to any one who calls you to account for the hope that is in you, yet do it with gentleness and reverence" (I Peter 3:15).

It is also theologically sound, for it circumvents the two major criticisms that are usually directed to those who are accused of arguing from personal experience, the problem of subjectivism and the problem of relativism. In response to the first objection, I maintain that the approach I am advocating answers it by redefining the subjective/objective dichotomy, which has traditionally defined experience as subjective. But I maintain that the facts of my experience are real. It is the meaning that I attach to them that is subjective. Granted that I evaluate my experience from the perspective of faith, the experience itself is objective. The unbelievers' evaluations of the same facts may be entirely different, but they are no less subjective. The unbelievers should confess their presuppositions, too, and then talk about the confirming evidence. In the process there will be better communication, if not agreement.

As for the charge of relativism, faith-sharing is not an attempt to impose one's experience on everyone else. The believers do not claim that their experiences are normative, but that they confirm their own beliefs. Until faith in God becomes a personal experience of God, it is not a conviction of the heart, but merely one's intellectual assent to an idea.

Faith-sharing recognizes the validity of "experiential religion," to use Richard R. Niebuhr's term. Our belief in God will lack power and appeal if it is not based on personal experience. The only legitimate statements about God are those which express an existential relationship with God.

Diogenes Allen, in his philosophical essay *The Reasonableness of Faith* (Corpus Books, 1968), makes an even stronger claim for personal experience. He argues that "whether or not a viable case for the truth of religious beliefs is available or becomes available, it is perfectly reasonable to continue to affirm religious beliefs on the basis of the needs which they satisfy" (p. xv).

Allen has provided a philosophical rationale for faith which comes to grips with modern thinking, including logical positivism and linguistic analysis. He rightly points out that the real challenge of logical positivism is not the verification principle, which states that no proposition is legitimate unless it can be subjected to verification or falsification by empirical evidence. It can easily be shown that such a principle does not rule out metaphysical or religious statements. The real challenge of the positivist point of view is the same old issue of demanding that there be empirical grounds for believing in God. "When proofs for God's existence, for example, are shown to be invalid, it is only a rationale that has been destroyed, not the actual ground for the adherence to belief in God" (p. 83). Allen's claim is that "the satisfaction of needs which motivate one to have faith in God is *a* solid ground for affirming religious truth-claims *without* logically depending on rationales for their truth" (p. 95).

It would follow, therefore, that making a case for God would mean sharing one's experiences of satisfied needs. This is also true psychologically, if the insights of the contemporary human potential movement are correct. From sensitivity training to transactional analysis the emphasis has been on verbalizing feelings and personal experiences. Thomas A. Harris, the popularizer of transactional analysis, in his best seller *I'm OK—You're OK* (Avon Books, 1973) asks: "Is there such a thing as a religious experience, or is such an experience simply a psychological aberration? Does the mind 'just get carried away' with a wish, as Freud suggested, or is there more to it than fantasy?" (p. 265). Using a T formation of Trueblood, Teilhard, and Tillich, Dr. Harris makes a case for "transcendence," which he defines as "an experience of that which is more than myself, a reality outside of myself, that which has been called The Other, The All, or God" (p. 267).

Harris then goes on to describe in the jargon of T.A.

what happens in a religious experience: "It is my opinion that religious experience may be a unique combination of Child (a feeling of intimacy) and Adult (a reflection on ultimacy) with the total exclusion of the Parent. . . . I believe the Adult's function in the religious experience is to block out the Parent in order that the Natural Child may reawaken to its own worth and beauty as a part of God's creation" (pp. 267–268).

"Early Christian literature," says Harris, "was essentially a report of what happened and what had been said. 'Once I was blind and now I see' is a statement of an experience and not an interesting theological idea. The early Christians met to talk about an exciting encounter, about having met a man, named Jesus, who walked with them, who laughed with them, who cried with them, and whose openness and compassion for people was a central historical example of *I'm OK—You're OK*" (pp. 268–270).

I have quoted from T. A. Harris' book not to endorse transactional analysis but to show that modern psychology, as represented by Harris and other exponents of the human potential movement, provides a further confirmation of the indispensable relation between faith and personal experience, and of the validity of talking about that experience to others (faith-sharing).

Practical experience also confirms what we have seen to be theoretically true from a Biblical, theological, philosophical, and psychological viewpoint. Those who make evangelistic calls discover that people respond much more readily and positively to a faith-sharing approach than to an intellectual rationale. Preachers find their congregations influenced more by personal illustrations than by powerful logic. One can describe one's own experience without threatening the other person. Sharing the evidences of God in one's own life does not put the other person on the defensive, but allows that person the freedom to assess the evidence and make his or her own application.

IV. CONCLUSION

If what has been said about faith-sharing is true, then the task of the evangelist is not to try to prove the existence of God in propositional terms, but rather to share one's experiences of satisfied needs. One can speak with authority about one's own experience, and one can do so in a way that is appealing, if not compelling. "That . . . which we have heard, which we have seen with our eyes, which we have looked upon and touched with our hands, concerning the word of life, . . . we proclaim also to you" (I John 1:1–3).

The difference between believers and unbelievers is a matter of who gets the credit. The believers look at life through the eyes of faith and interpret their experiences in the light of their understanding of God. They are always ready, as Peter exhorts us to be, to give a reason for the hope that is within them. Their object is to win people, not arguments, and they try to do it by sharing their faith when it is opportune and appropriate to do so.

As Christian witnesses and evangelists, then, our task is not to prove that Jesus Christ is the Son of God. That we can never do. Our task is to show by the way we speak and act that we believe he is. That, by God's grace, we can do!

3

A Servant Church

We show with integrity our belief in Jesus Christ as the Son of God if we ask ourselves what it means to be Christ's man or Christ's woman in the world today. The answer to that question defines the quality of our discipleship; and when church members take it seriously, the church will truly become a servant church.

If there is one image in the Bible that expresses the mission of the church, it is that of a servant. In the Old Testament book of Isaiah, Israel was exhorted to realize that God was calling his people to be a servant people, that their role was not to be one of privilege without responsibility, but that they were called to glorify their Lord. "You are my servant, Israel, in whom I will be glorified" (Isa. 49:3).

I. THE SUFFERING SERVANT

The people of Israel were anxiously hoping for the long-awaited appearance of their Messiah. They thought of him as a political hero, a strong-armed prince whom God would send to establish them as a mighty nation. But in Isaiah (ch. 53), the message was that the Messiah would come not as a king, but as a suffering servant, with "no form or comeliness . . . and no beauty that we should desire him." He would be despised and rejected by men, a man of sorrows and acquainted with grief, wounded for our transgressions, bruised for our iniquities, oppressed and afflicted.

When at last the Messiah, the Christ, did come, he appeared as a suffering servant. As Paul says, he "emptied himself, taking the form of a servant" (Phil. 2:7). In order that his disciples might grasp the significance of this, Jesus humbled himself before them by washing their feet. "You call me Teacher and Lord," he said; "and you are right, for so I am. If I then, your Lord and Teacher, have washed your feet, you also ought to wash one another's feet. For I have given you an example, that you also should do as I have done to you" (John 13:13–15).

II. OUR CHIEF END

Our destiny as Christians, then, is to become, like Paul, servants of Jesus Christ. Our chief end, as the Westminster Shorter Catechism reminds us, "is to glorify God, and to enjoy him forever."

That does not mean we are to revel in being children of God, jealously clinging to our select status as members of the Christian church, and patting ourselves on the back for our good fortune. This is the danger of that extreme brand of evangelical Christianity which makes the church community an end in itself. To glorify God, we must reveal his nature and purpose to all mankind, by our words and deeds. That was the message that came to the people of Israel through the book of Isaiah. The Lord said, "It is too light a thing that you should be my servant to raise up the tribes of Jacob and to restore the preserved of Israel; I will give you as a light to the nations, that my salvation may reach to the end of the earth" (Isa. 49:6).

The church exists to glorify God and it glorifies God by being his witness, a light to the world. In the Sermon on the Mount, Jesus said, "Let your light so shine before men, that they may see your good works and give glory to your Father who is in heaven" (Matt. 5:16).

As Christians we glorify God in order that he may be glorified by others. What we as members of the church do and say affects what others think about him who is the head of the church, Jesus Christ. We are not going to win many disciples for Christ if our actions deny the faith we profess with our lips.

In order to be true to itself and faithful to its God-given mission, the church must be the instrument of God's glory. Jesus established a fellowship of which he himself was the very core and the source of power. He commissioned the disciples to spread the good news throughout all the earth. "All authority in heaven and on earth has been given to me," he told them. "Go therefore and make disciples of all nations" (Matt. 28:18–19).

The dynamic force in the church is the Spirit of the risen Christ. "You shall receive power when the Holy Spirit has come upon you; and you shall be my witnesses" (Acts 1:8). Where Christ is, there is a church that is alive and vital. We follow a living Lord, not a dead martyr. As one gospel song puts it, "I serve a risen Savior, he's in the world today." Jesus said: "Because I live, you will live also" (John 14:19). "He who believes in me will also do the works that I do; and greater works than these will he do" (John 14:12).

The church was established by the grace of Christ to be a means of grace for his followers. It was for the church that he instituted the sacraments, and it is in the church that we partake of them. It was to the church that he promised the gift of the Holy Spirit. It was the church which he commanded to be his witness by word and by deed. It was for the church that he died.

III. A TWOFOLD MISSION

The mission of the church, then, is to be the institution, divinely established, in which the God and Father of Jesus Christ is made real to people. The mission is twofold.

The first part is to develop and nurture its own members. The members of a servant church must surely serve one another. The Bible says, "exhort one another" (Heb. 3:13), "comfort one another" (I Thess. 4:18), "love one another" (I Peter 1:22), "bear one another's burdens" (Gal. 6:2). This is what is meant by Christian fellowship. This is part of our mission, to be a fellowship, in which there is mutual give-and-take.

It is in this fellowship that members are able to exercise spiritual discipline, under the inspiration of Christ, through the means of prayer, the sacraments, the preaching of the word, diligent reading of the Scriptures, pastoral care, observing the ordinances, and all other phases of Christian life. From start to finish discipline is a function of fellowship. Paul said, "Be subject to one another out of reverence for Christ" (Eph. 5:21). His words are echoed by Peter, "Likewise you that are younger be subject to the elders. Clothe yourselves, all of you, with humility toward one another" (I Peter 5:5).

So part of the mission of a servant church is to be a fellowship in which the individual members can grow. Can we find a better expression of this than that by Paul in his letter to the Ephesians? "And he gave gifts to men . . . and his gifts were that some should be apostles, some prophets, some evangelists, some pastors and teachers, to equip the saints for the work of ministry, for building up the body of Christ, until we all attain to the unity of the faith and of the knowledge of the Son of God, to mature manhood, to the measure of the stature of the fulness of Christ" (Eph. 4:8, 11–13).

The second part of the twofold mission of the church is to carry the good news to all men. "Go into all the world and preach the gospel to the whole creation" (Mark 16:15). It was Paul who so clearly saw this task of the church and devoted his life to it. "To me, though I am the very least of all the saints, this grace was given, to preach to the Gentiles the unsearchable riches of Christ, and to make all men see what is the plan" (Eph. 3:8–9). Paul even gives the church a cosmic dimension when he says, "This grace was given, . . . that through the church the manifold wisdom of God might now be made known to the principalities and powers in the heavenly places" (Eph. 3:8, 10).

IV. A THREEFOLD FUNCTION

In carrying out its mission to glorify God before mankind and to be a witness, the church has a threefold function.

First, *it has a prophetic function:* to speak to the world for God. The church must bear witness to the word of God, which is eternal and everlasting, and yet completely contemporary and relevant. For the word of God speaks to every age and every time. But as a historical community the church must interpret the gospel to its own age.

In the day of Nazi tyranny members of the Confessional Church of Germany issued the famous Declaration of Barmen, in which they said that their supreme loyalty was to Christ and not to the State. Martin Niemoeller and many others were thrown into concentration camps. They were modern prophets. A servant church's role in society is constantly to criticize and evaluate the contemporary culture in the light of God's revelation.

To do this, we need intelligent Christian thinkers, people who understand their faith and can look at the human situation from a Christian perspective. This means the church must fulfill its teaching responsibility. Revelation is not enough; we need sound theology. A faith that is not intellectually respectable will not be adequate for today's world.

It is not that the church has a ready-made solution to all the world's needs. A Christian does not have all the answers to the problems that beset mankind. Being a Christian does not make one an expert in economics, or medicine, or politics, or international relations, or business, or

managing a household, or anything else. What the world
needs is not spiritual jacks-of-all-trades, but Christian men
and women who will practice their faith in their daily
lives. The world needs *Christian* statesmen, doctors, law-
yers, businessmen, teachers, housewives. It is the church
upon whose shoulders falls the task of helping men and
women to be Christians-on-the-job. This is the teaching
function of the church, and it must be faithfully carried
out if the church is to exercise its prophetic role in society.

Since the church exists because of Christ's missionary
command, the mark of a true church is its missionary character. That's not just emotional ardor, but genuine dedica-
tion. Many people can talk a good game, but that's not the
real test of our faith. The early disciples were not mere
talkers. They gave themselves completely to a cause. The
true church is one that belongs to a cause. It has life only
to the extent that it gives itself away. "Whoever loses his
life for my sake," said Jesus, "will find it" (Matt. 16:25). The
church is a representative community, which belongs not
to itself, but to a mission. We don't give purpose to ourselves; we give ourselves to a purpose. All of this has to do
with the church's prophetic role.

Second, *the church also has a priestly function,* in
which it exercises its role in mediating the redeeming love
of God. The church can do this because it is a "remembering community." This note of remembrance is seen
throughout the entire Bible. In the Old Testament the
people of Israel were constantly reminded of what God
had done for them. "I am the Lord your God, who brought
you out of the land of Egypt, out of the house of bondage"
(Ex. 20:2).

We as Christians remember what Christ has done for all
humankind. Remembering is an important service that
the church renders humanity, for it keeps us from the
illusion of self-sufficiency and pride.

A servant church should be one community where
every person is taken seriously, where a human being is

treated as a total personality. A man or a woman is not just a consumer to be persuaded, a voter to be won, a worker to be counted, a brain to be harnessed. A person is not just a statistic, but is a unique individual. Christ looked upon men and women as persons whose lives needed wholeness and meaning. The true church is this kind of community because it has this kind of Lord.

The church has no monopoly on goodness, but it is the community of forgiveness. It is through the church that people are made aware of God's love and his great act of redemption. And it is the mission of the church to mediate that love and redemption to all the world.

How? By manifesting the Spirit of the gospel in our relationships with all those in need of deliverance, whether it be from sin or sickness or any other kind of suffering. A servant church must take the lead in providing relief for victims of disaster from flood, fire, earthquake, or storm; the church must be concerned for the poverty-stricken, the sick, the homeless, the hungry, the disadvantaged, the oppressed. A servant church must have a broad perspective in its concern for social justice and all other aspects of human relations. The church must continue to pioneer in all fields, working unceasingly and relentlessly toward a better world. By the church we mean every professing Christian, as well as local congregations, and denominations, and the church universal. This is the redemptive function of the church.

Third, *the church has a communal function,* which is to pursue the unity of Christ and to bring all people into the fellowship of believers. As long as there is schism and bitterness and rivalry among the different churches, we are denying our fundamental nature, which is to be united in Christ. This does not mean that we must seek to do away with denominations, but rather that we should recognize our common allegiance to one Lord and not let differences of structure and form split the body of Christ. There is room for differences in church government, in liturgical

practices, in theological emphases. We can learn from one
another.

The Christian church was established for a purpose: to
carry the gospel to all parts of the world and to draw all
people unto Christ. This is its mission, and every local
congregation is part of that mission. The church that is not
a missionary church is not a servant church. That does not
mean simply sending out fraternal workers to foreign
lands, although that's important, to be sure. But there are
mission frontiers right in our own backyard, frontiers of
thought as well as geography. There are frontiers in the
world of science, education, business, politics, athletics,
international relations, even in that of religion.

V. ON THIS ROCK

What are we doing to open up the frontier that we call
our parish? What are we doing to bring the message of
Christ to the community which God has called us to serve?
Reflecting on such questions may cause us to feel discouraged if not guilty, until we remember Jesus' response
to Peter's great affirmation of faith. When Peter declared,
"You are the Christ, the Son of the living God," Jesus
replied, "Blessed are you, Simon Bar-Jona! For flesh and
blood has not revealed this to you, but my Father who is
in heaven. And I tell you, you are Peter, and on this rock
I will build my church" (Matt. 16:16–18).

Some might think Jesus should have said, "On this rock
I will shipwreck my church." Christians have been so
hung up on that rock for so many centuries that they have
neglected the positive thrust of the oft-quoted passage. My
intention is not to debate the various interpretations that
have been applied to it. I want to focus on the tremendous
claim which Jesus makes that the powers of death, or the
gates of hell, as the King James Version translates the
phrase, shall not prevail against the church. I take it Jesus
is talking about the corporate fellowship, the body of be-

lievers who bear his name, the worshiping, working, witnessing community, the institutional church, if you will. "The gates of hell," said Jesus, "shall not prevail against it."

It is important to note that this positive affirmation of the church by Jesus was spoken in response to Peter's personal confession of faith in him! That fact in itself should be enough to remind us that a commitment to Jesus Christ implies a commitment also to the church of which Jesus is the builder and Lord. There can be no separation between our loyalty to Christ and our loyalty to the church for which Christ died.

The image that Jesus used in his remark to Peter has a two-directional application. If we think of it as *the powers of death,* as the Revised Standard Version translates the phrase, then we have the church as the invincible society, the mighty fortress, which death itself cannot destroy. But if we follow the King James Version and use the expression *the gates of hell,* we form a different mental picture. Here it is the church that is on the attack. Gates do not attack. Gates are what must be attacked. The church is on the offensive here, and the gates of hell, says Jesus, shall not prevail against it.

VI. A COMMISSION

Whatever the proper exegesis, the point is clear: the church and the legions of hell should be in conflict, not in cahoots. I like the second image and I see it as a commission for the church, for it implies that the church of which Jesus Christ is the builder must storm the gates of hell. This is truly an appropriate commission for our day and age, when there are so many hellish gates all about us. Here is our call to involvement, our call to be where the action is, to be wherever the fires of our man-made hells are burning.

There are many hells. War is hell, as General Sherman said, and so is poverty, and hunger, and disease, and slav-

ery, whatever form it takes. And so is pollution, whose
hellish flames may be the greatest challenge to our sur-
vival on this planet. Crime and corruption, immorality,
racism, violence, lawlessness, and oppression—the fires of
hell blaze all around us, casting on the curtains that frame
our brief moment on the stage of history their gruesome
shadows of man's inhumanity to man.

Now is the time for those of us who call ourselves
Christians to take our stand for what is right in God's
sight, for what is decent, and fair, and just, and health-
ful, and wholesome, and good, and true. We who are
called to be Christ's men and women in the world
today must proclaim our faith by word and by deed in
ways that will communicate to this jet-propelled age in
which we live. That means responding to needs, not
just reacting to demands. The call is to action, not *reaction*. Our Lord came as a suffering servant, and we are
called to be a servant church.

What, then, does it mean to be the servant church in the
world today? It means that:

wherever there is conflict, there the church must be as
an instrument of reconciliation;

wherever there is injustice, there the church must be as
an agent of reform;

wherever there is suffering or want, there the church
must be as a community of compassion, ministering to the
needs of people in whatever ways are possible;

wherever there is corruption, there the church must be
as a symbol of God's judgment on the evils of society and
as a witness to his truth;

wherever person is separated from person, group from
group, race from race, nation from nation, there the
church must be as a demonstration of God's love and of
our oneness in Jesus Christ.

We should have learned by now that if we are ever
going to change the corporate power structures that have

enslaved and tyrannized humankind, if we are ever going to reform the system itself, we will have to take seriously the corporate dimensions of the church's mission and ministry.

VII. AN ENDORSEMENT

The church cannot storm the gates of hell unless and until the church is willing to go to hell, for Christ's sake. That's what he did for us. And when his people are open to the leading of the Holy Spirit, they can batter down the gates of many a hell, for Jesus' statement to Peter was not just a commission; it was also an endorsement of the church. I believe it, because I have seen it happen. I have witnessed the impact that a local church can have on its community when its members are not afraid to take their stand for justice and truth. This truth was dramatically illustrated by the faithful leaders of the Oak Lane Presbyterian Church, leaders whose forthright stand against the bitter opposition of some of their fellow members enabled that congregation to prove that it was possible to be a genuinely integrated church in a racially changing community.

There are those who say that the church has failed, that the gates of hell have already prevailed. This is said not just by atheistic communists, cynics, and skeptics. It is being said by many people who love the church, but who sincerely believe the church has lost its power, that it is no longer a viable institution. They see the typical church as a hodgepodge of unessential activities and meaningless busywork, a social club for pseudo-pious part-timers who meet to eat and eat to meet.

They think the church is irrelevant, and too often they are right. It is true that churches have failed many times and will continue to fail, because churches are people and people fail. But God is not so ready to give up on his people as some of us are. We are too quick to criticize and condemn. We rule people out of the kingdom because they don't measure up to our image of a Christian. We label them and toss them into the bin with our collection of rejects, be they theological, or ecclesiastical, or social, or political, or racial, or moral rejects. How wrong we are, when we do this!

For all the imperfections.of its members, for all its faults and failures, the church is still the church of Christ. He is still the Lord of the church. He is the builder. Maybe his workers are not what they ought to be; unskilled laborers at best we are. But by his grace great things can happen, great things *do* happen, when we are willing to let the church be the church, when we are willing to let Jesus Christ *be* the Lord of the church.

Some of us ministers need to be reminded of this, because in our zeal to reform the world, we lose sight of the realities of life. To use a familiar metaphor, we go charging up the hill on our own personal crusade, and we get so far out in front that we are mistaken for the enemy. That is the best way to get shot in the back by one of our own troops. We forget that people are people, and we have to take them as they are, and work with them as they are, and *love* them as they are. That's what Jesus did. "Christ loved the church and gave himself up for her." What greater endorsement could there be than that?

VIII. A PROMISE

If we are willing to do the same, then the church will not fail, for Jesus' statement to Peter is not only a commission for the church and an endorsement of the church, it is also a promise to the church. The gates of hell *shall* not prevail —future tense!

I see signs that Jesus' promise is being kept even in our time. I am not saying that the denouement has begun, that the Last Days are upon us. I am saying that there are plenty of signs that "there's life in the old gal yet," that the church is still on the attack, and the gates of hell will not ultimately prevail.

One sign for me has been the response of so many churches to a new style of evangelism that takes into account the social dimensions of the gospel. Along with that there is a new awareness of and emphasis upon the need for personal commitment. We have the younger generation largely to thank for this development.

Another sign is the new ecumenical spirit which has emerged in recent years, a spirit that goes far beyond the old cooperative worship services on Thanksgiving Day. It is reflected in a greater appreciation of and respect for the beliefs of other religions.

Still another sign of Jesus' promise is that exciting things are happening in churches all across the country—new forms of worship, new methods of teaching, new arenas of ministry, imaginative and creative programs of all kinds.

One more indication is that God is still calling men and women, young and older, into his service. The Holy Spirit is still at work in the hearts of people, and as long as that is true, the gates of hell shall not prevail.

These are but a few of the signs I see that Jesus' promise to Peter is being kept. I know there are many things wrong with the world today. There are many, many problems and many, many institutions and agencies trying to solve them. But I believe that the church of Jesus Christ is still the most powerful force for good in the world. That is not just a theoretical observation; that is a conviction based on my own experience in the local church.

One of the main thrusts of our ministry, then, is to help the people we serve to understand themselves to be the servant people of God, whose mission is to minister not only to one another but to the community as well, to meet the needs of people both within and without the walls of the church. But how do we help a church to see the need? And how do we motivate and equip a church to meet the need? The purpose of service evangelism is to do just that.

4

Service Evangelism

Too few churches are ready to accept their evangelistic responsibilities. A few years ago I was conducting workshops, seminars, and conferences for pastors and lay people from many different denominations. I was led to conclude that Mr. and Mrs. Average Church Member were not at all excited about evangelism. The word itself turned them off. They were not at all sure that this was something in which their church should be involved. "After all," they reasoned, "we live in a pluralistic society. What right do we Christians have to impose our faith upon anyone else? It is certainly not something which I as a Christian feel any obligation to be involved in, even if someone could convince me that some Christians ought to be doing it. Get somebody else, because I'm neither Biblically nor theologically equipped for anything like that."

I found myself continually having to make a case for evangelism. This was dramatically illustrated during a workshop which I was asked to conduct in Rochester, New York, at the 1971 General Assembly of The United Presbyterian Church U.S.A. The room assigned us was jam-packed from wall to wall, with people crowding around the doors and in the hallways. They were attracted by the topic, which at that point in history was even more controversial an issue than the hotly debated contribution to the Angela Davis Defense Fund. It soon became apparent that many had come to the workshop not to share ideas but to fight. Within a few minutes we were divided into two camps, with the social activists and the personal salvationists hurling their choicest epithets at each other.

There we were, a microcosm of the church, exemplifying what every thoughtful Christian knows is a false but real dichotomy. What an opportunity for us to try to reconcile two emphases that should be complementary rather than mutually exclusive. Two hours later we had succeeded in doing just that, at least for most of us in the room. We began to agree upon a concept of evangelism that included both personal commitment and social concern. It seems so obvious that it should not be either/or but both/and, yet I find it never goes without saying, for even today people tend to identify themselves and others with one side or the other.

In every workshop or seminar people would bring their preconceived notions of what evangelism is and where other people are in relation to it. Their stereotyped concepts of evangelism were an inevitable obstacle that had to be dealt with at the outset of every training session. Before I could make a case for "doing" evangelism, we had to define what evangelism is. And how much time we spent in the process! I might have said wasted, had I not realized that there was some value in helping people to broaden their understanding of a subject that had been so long neglected in the church. People were now talking about evangelism. They were still not *doing* anything about it, but at least they were discussing it!

As time wore on, discussion seemed to be for some a substitute for action. Many were turned off by the more aggressive, propositional approaches that were becoming popular and producing spectacular results in terms of membership growth in some churches. Although I did not identify with the theology of such approaches, I liked what they were doing much better than what their critics were not doing!

The training P.R.O.O.F. model is actually a seminar on the nature and meaning of faith. The purpose is to explore the meaning of faith, in a way the average church member can understand, to experience the reality of faith, and to establish a method of sharing faith. In the process the participants should discover if they believe, why they believe, and what they believe, and so become more effective ambassadors for Christ.

The faith probe is itself an extremely valuable experience for deepening the spiritual life of those who participate. Those who have attended the P.R.O.O.F. seminars have come out feeling more confident and competent in communicating their faith. The training method of P.R.O.O.F. would be helpful regardless of the evangelistic approach a church might use, but it is particularly suited to what I am calling service evangelism.

By evangelism I mean reaching out to others in Christian love, identifying with them, caring for them, listening to them, and sharing one's faith with them in such a way that they will freely respond and want to commit themselves to trust, love, and obey God as a disciple of Jesus Christ and a member of his servant community, the church. That, I realize, is a statement of method as well as my definition of evangelism. The word "service" is intended to imply a style of evangelism that is caring, supportive, unselfish, sensitive, and responsive to human need. It is evangelism done by a servant church, whose people are there not to be served but to serve.

In a P.R.O.O.F. seminar we spend some time in small groups considering various definitions and in developing our own, after which I take some time to elaborate on my own definition, by pointing out several distinctions that need to be kept in mind.

I. THE WORD ITSELF AND HOW WE USE IT

We need to be clear about the various ways we use the word "evangelism." Much of the disagreement arises from the failure to distinguish between the meaning and the means. That is to say, we confuse our definition with our concept of method. We mentally picture someone grabbing us by the lapels and shouting, "Are you saved?" and we say, "I don't believe in evangelism." But what we are rejecting is the way it is done, not what it means. There is a distinction between the medium and the message. Many arguments could be avoided if those involved would stop confusing what evangelism is with the way it is done. If you have any doubt about this point, check it out the next time you encounter someone who is against evangelism. See if the reason for antagonism is not related to the concept of how it is done. If so, the meaning is being confused with the means.

A second source of confusion in our use of the word "evangelism" is our failure to distinguish between the setting and the style. In a given situation some evangelistic styles are appropriate and some are not. Just as we need to coordinate the what and the way, so do we need to coordinate the where and the how. There is an appropriate style for every setting. In some situations the best approach may be to *speak up* for Christ, while in others it may be to *shut up,* for his sake! The fact that some people do not relate their style to the setting is not a valid reason for rejecting all evangelism.

Still another source of confusion is the failure to distinguish between evangelism and what George Sweazey refers to as "pre-evangelism." We hear people say: "I witness by the way I live. I don't have to talk about it." What they are doing is confusing moral conduct with evangelism, the law with the gospel. Moslems, Jews, Buddhists, secular humanists, and atheists all can bear that kind of witness.

But that is not evangelism. Where is the gospel? Life-style without reference to Christ is not evangelism. At best it is only a preliminary step (pre-evangelism). Sooner or later the word must be spoken. "Always be prepared to make a defense" (I Peter 3:15).

It is true that people witness by the way they live, as well as by what they say. But when you think about it, is it not rather arrogant for one to claim to lead people to Christ by one's own virtuousness? "I'll show them I'm a Christian by the way I live!" Oh, will you? And what kind of Christian is that? How many people even know you are a Christian? How can they know if you don't tell them? Non-Christians can be "good," too! Some of them are "gooder" than many Christians. That raises the question of the relationship between evangelism and witnessing.

II. Evangelism and Witnessing

There are several terms that occur frequently in evangelistic jargon and that are sometimes confused. We need to understand, first of all, the difference between a witness and an advocate. There is a popular question that has been going the rounds for a number of years: If you were on trial for being a Christian, would there be enough evidence to convict you? That question challenges your Christian witness. I have suggested, however, a quite different question: If Jesus Christ were on trial today (and he still is!), would he want you for his lawyer? That question challenges your ability as an advocate!

Witnessing is telling what we have heard and seen; advocacy is making a case. Witnessing is testifying; advocacy is defending. We also "witness" (i.e., show our faith) by the way we live, including how we speak. For that reason we are witnesses when we advocate, but we are not necessarily advocates when we witness.

Two other terms that need to be clarified are evidence and testimony. Evidence is that which supports our case, or to put it theologically, that which confirms our faith assumptions. Testimony is what we say when we bear witness. When one gives a personal testimony, one may tell what is believed or describe a conversion experience, or share one's faith. Whatever is said is testimony, and whatever evidence is cited to support the statement may or may not be convincing.

Evangelism involves all of the above—witnessing, advocacy, evidence, and testimony—but is neither equated with nor limited to any or all of them. I may "witness" to a fellow Christian, but that is not evangelism. I may share my personal testimony with an adult Bible class, and neither is that evangelism. The terms are not mutually exclusive, but they mean different things and the distinctions should be kept in mind.

III. Evangelism and the Evangelical

The word "evangelical," like the word "evangelism," means different things to different people. Technically speaking, evangelical means "belonging to, contained in, agreeable to, or in the spirit of the gospel or the teachings of the New Testament." To some people an evangelical is a person who stresses the importance of a personal relationship with Jesus Christ. An evangelical preacher is "one who preaches the gospel and whose sermons are Christ-centered." It implies the comfortable use of traditional God language and Biblical terms such as sin, judgment, salvation, eternal life. It is sometimes used as a derogatory label by those who view evangelicals as too pietistic, individualistic, and irrelevant. But there are those who call themselves evangelical liberals, who seek to keep a balance between personal faith and social action. It is interesting that even those who despise "evangelicals" believe themselves to be evangelical. Whether it is meant as a compliment or a criticism depends upon who is using the term and about whom! We shall return to that point in a moment, but for now we need to understand the term "evangelical" in relation to evangelism.

Evangelism, strictly speaking, refers to the proclamation or promulgation of the gospel, "the good news." A distinction between the two terms is necessary because it is possible for people and churches to be evangelical without being evangelistic. They can speak evangelically to one another, without being engaged in promulgating the gospel to the world about them. Evangelical implies a theological emphasis, whereas evangelism implies a purposeful activity. Evangelical is being; evangelism is doing.

The distinction is important and valid, but a Christian should not be one or the other, but should be both. For churches as well as for individuals it is not an either/or but a both/and responsibility. That responsibility can be and must be exercised without diminishing the emphasis on social action. There must be a balance if the gospel is to be proclaimed with integrity.

IV. EVANGELISM AND COMMUNICATION

We should recognize the obvious truth that proclaiming the gospel and communicating the gospel are two different things. Does the fact that it is proclaimed necessarily mean that it is heard? Does the fact that it is heard mean that it is understood? Does the fact that it is understood mean that it is believed? Does the fact that it is believed mean that it is followed? Does it matter?

Evangelism assumes that it does matter. The church recognizes that proclamation is a necessary and valid form of evangelism, but it cannot assume that just because the gospel has been proclaimed, communication has taken place. Christians have too often been guilty of thinking that because it has been said it has been heard, and because it has been heard it has been understood. What good does it do to proclaim the gospel in English to a German-speaking audience that does not understand English? Or in English to an English-speaking audience that cannot understand the concepts? Proclamation has its place, but communication is the goal, whatever form it takes.

V. EVANGELISM AND SOCIAL ACTION

Most people agree theoretically with the need for a balance between evangelism and social action. The terms are not mutually exclusive. Yet the adherents of each often act as if they are, and the reason for the animosity between the two camps is the false images that each side has of the other. The love of Christ constrains us to be concerned about and to serve others. As a servant community, the local church exists to minister to the needs of people, and in so doing, the church must serve the whole person—physical as well as spiritual needs—just as the churches of the New Testament did, not to mention Jesus and his disciples. But people live in a social context, and they are affected by the pressures and problems of society. To be involved in their lives is therefore to be concerned about the social, political, and economic problems that affect their lives.

Social action, therefore, is the natural consequence of service evangelism, but not vice versa. It is possible to be meaningfully involved in social action without being involved in evangelism, as countless secular organizations and government agencies are. But it is not possible, in my opinion, to be meaningfully involved in *service* evangelism without being involved in social action. An evangelistic approach that is truly concerned with reaching the whole person, I repeat, cannot overlook the social dimension of a person's life, or the context in which that life is lived.

The rejection by some of social action as a valid expression of Christian faith stems partly from a lack of understanding of the meaning of personal faith. Faith in Jesus Christ is strictly personal. For some people that means,

"It's none of your business." A personal relationship with Christ means to them: "It's nobody's business what Jesus and I have going between us. I don't have to share it; I don't have to relate to anyone else in the process." That is what I mean by private, not personal. Strictly personal does not mean strictly private.

Nor does it mean strictly individualistic. To say that Christian faith is strictly personal does not mean that it is nonsocial. The age-old controversy between personal faith and social action is, always has been, and always will be a false dichotomy. There can be no separation between these two equally valid dimensions of religious experience. They are two sides of the same coin. To say that faith is strictly personal does not mean that it has nothing to do with the world and its needs, problems, issues, and challenges. It has everything to do with all of those.

Nevertheless, it is strictly personal, because it has to do with a God who is personal, and who has revealed himself through a person, whom we believe to be the Christ. We speak of God in a personal way. We use a personal pronoun. God is not the conclusion of a philosophical argument. God is not an idea, a theory, a notion. God is not a thing, an object we can hold in the palm of our hands. God is not a personality, but is personal in the sense that God is a responsive reality to whom we are responsible and with whom we can have a personal relationship. We cannot relate to an abstraction. We cannot be responsible to an it. God is not an it. God is personal.

But as John reminds us, no one has ever seen God. That is where Jesus comes in. The Christian believes that God has revealed himself to humankind in Jesus Christ. "The only Son," we are told in the first chapter of John, "who is in the bosom of the Father, he has made him known" (John 1:18). We know what God is like because he revealed himself in a person. If we want to know God, we must get to know Jesus, who lived and taught on earth. Christianity focuses on the person of Jesus Christ.

Christian faith is personal, therefore, because it is about a person. It is personal, secondly, because it is transmitted through persons. Christianity is a person-to-person religion. Everything we know about our faith, everything we hear, every word we read about Christ, is the result of personal activity. The Bible is the product of persons who were inspired by the Holy Spirit to write what they wrote, and we would not have it if other persons had not been inspired by the Holy Spirit to say that this book is inspired. It took hundreds of years for the canon to be identified, and if it had not been for the church, which is a community of persons, the doctrines of faith would not have been hammered out so that the gospel and all of its implications could be understandable to persons.

If it were not for persons, there would be no teaching, no preaching, no sacraments, no proclamation of the gospel, no witness to the person of Jesus Christ. In short, there would be no Christianity. God could have found another way to communicate his truth, which he was and is perfectly free to do and perfectly capable of doing, but in the context of our experience, Christianity as we know it today would be impossible without persons. Jesus told the woman of Samaria about God. The woman told her fellow Samaritans about Jesus. That is the way it goes. Christianity is a religion about a person, from persons.

But it is more. It is *for* persons. The woman of Samaria is a beautiful example of what can and should happen to us. Having been confronted by the person of Christ, what did she do? Did she keep it to herself? Did she tell the people: "It's none of your business what happened to me! That's my private affair"? No, she was so excited that she could not wait to tell everyone she saw that she had met a man who knew everything about her. "Can this be the Christ?" (John 4:29).

Christianity is a religion to be shared with others, not only with those who already know Jesus but also with those who have not known him. This is our evangelistic responsibility. Someone has commented that too many Christians share their faith with one another and have fellowship with the world, when it ought to be the other way around!

Remember who these people were that the woman went back to tell. They were not Jews. They were Samaritans, people whom the Jews despised. Jews had no dealings with Samaritans. Jesus was in foreign territory, on enemy turf, a stranger among people presumably opposed to everything he represented. But the Samaritan woman was so turned on by her encounter with him that she went back to share it with her fellow townspeople. And of all things, they responded with equal enthusiasm! They hurried off to find Jesus and beg him to stay with them. This he did for two days, teaching and preaching and sharing himself with them, these social undesirables whom the Jews despised. What a contrast between these people, who were supposed to hate Jesus and yet received him gladly, and the people of Nazareth, his own hometown, who should have loved him but were offended by his words and wanted to throw him over a cliff!

What does this have to say about our evangelistic thrust and about our social involvement, our relation to the world? Remember, Jesus Christ is for the world, not just for us who call ourselves Christians, not just for those who have made some kind of verbal commitment, but for the whole world. Again it is John who reminds us that God so loved the *world*, that he gave his only Son . . . that the *world* might be saved through him.

This Christian faith which we sometimes wear on our sleeves with such great pride, but which is ours only by the grace of the God who has called us into it, is not meant to be private and is not meant to be nonsocial. To be a Christian is to be involved in and concerned about every single issue of society, speaking to the world of which we are a part, relating to it, working to make it better, this world which has so many needs and problems, so many faults and failures. It is precisely because Christianity is strictly personal that it must be social, and it is wrong to say, indeed it is unchristian to say, that Christian faith has nothing to do with social action. When we understand what it means to be Christ's man or woman, then we shall understand what it means to be sent into the world, as he sent his disciples into the world. Christianity is strictly personal because it is a religion for persons.

But most important of all, Christian faith is personal because it is a relationship with a person. Christianity is a personal relationship with Jesus Christ. How many times that has been said! But how many times has it been heard? Each one must discover this relationship for oneself, in one's own way, with one's own experience brought to bear upon it, in whatever context it may occur. No two persons necessarily have the same Christian experience. One person's encounter with Christ may be by a well. Another's may be in a church pew. One person's may come early, another's later in life. But come it must in a personal way, as illustrated so forcefully in the comment of the Samaritans to the woman, when they said, "It is no longer because of your words that we believe, for we have heard for ourselves, and we know that this is indeed the Savior of the world!" (John 4:42).

When we stop talking about God and start talking to God, then we can say our faith is strictly personal. When the words of others become Christ's word to me personally, then my religion is strictly personal. When the Jesus we have heard about becomes the Christ we know personally, then we can understand why he said, "I am the way, and the truth, and the life; no one comes to the Father, but by me" (John 14:6). When our worship is no longer mere ritual, but rather a relationship with the God and Father of our Lord Jesus Christ, then we will know what it means to worship in spirit and in truth, and our faith will truly be personal.

And when our faith is truly personal, we will understand

that the connection between evangelism and social action is a both/and, not an either/or relationship. We can never take it for granted, however, that people understand and accept that relationship, especially those who are inclined to favor one side over against the other. We who realize that faith is both personal and social, not private and individualistic, should not permit the dichotomy to go unchallenged, whenever we encounter it.

VI. EVANGELISM AND PROSELYTIZING

Once the relationship between evangelism and social action is understood, another distinction must be made. That is the difference between evangelism and proselytizing. The latter term means to convert a person from one religious belief to another, but I am using it in a pejorative sense to suggest a difference in style and purpose from service evangelism. The primary aim of service evangelism is to minister to people's needs, including, of course, their spiritual needs. Their beliefs may change in the process, but their faith in God should always be respected and affirmed.

The difference is a matter of emphasis. Service evangelism is concerned about persons; proselytizing is concerned about converts. Service evangelism is in no sense a compromise of one's Christian convictions. On the contrary, whatever one does, one does it in the name of the Christ who calls us to feed the hungry, and clothe the naked, and visit the sick, and welcome strangers, in short, to be concerned about people. But how different is the attitude of those proselytizers whose chief purpose is to add more notches to their spiritual gun butts! Their aim is not service but conquest.

Service evangelism is ecumenical in spirit. Proselytizing is anything but. Service evangelism does not insult the sincere adherents of other faiths by making dogmatic claims about Christianity. Nor does it treat them as heathen, an attitude that characterized much of our Western missionary activity for too many centuries. It is not bent on condemning loyal Jews to hell because they have not accepted Jesus as the Messiah.

This does not mean that evangelists have to conceal their own beliefs, but because they understand that their own faith is a gift they share it with humility. Evangelists recognize that they and their devout Jewish or Moslem friends worship the same God. The difference is Jesus Christ, in and through whom Christians believe God has offered a fuller revelation of his purpose and will than in any other religion, though there are parallels to and hints of the gospel in other faiths. Christian evangelists should always be looking for these points of contact, embracing truth wherever it is encountered, and inviting those with whom they enter into dialogue to consider Jesus as the answer to humankind's universal quest for salvation.

True evangelists are certainly not interested in turning Methodists into Presbyterians, or Episcopalians into Baptists, or Roman Catholics into Protestants. There are more than enough secular agnostics and totally unchurched, irreligious people in our society to keep evangelists busy. The kingdom of Christ is not advanced a single inch by proselytizing members from other churches, and we do Christ and his church a disservice by encouraging people to hop from one church to another. The rock on which Jesus said he would build his church was a solid rock, not a rolling stone. One trouble with the church today is that there are too many rolling stones, too many church shoppers, church hoppers, and church droppers.

Service evangelism is motivated by a genuine interest in others, not by self-interest. The purpose is to be a friend, not to gain a statistic. It is not, "What can they do for our church?" but "What can our church do for them?" That requires listening more than telling. The approach is incarnational rather than propositional. It is a matter of

being there and caring, instead of going there and unload-
ing.

What is needed is empathy, not polemics. We cannot
argue people into the kingdom! It is not a matter of making the other person agree with what I think or believe to
be true. What do I have if I succeed? Someone who believes what I believe! The task of evangelism is not per-
suading to a point of view, but pointing to a person, Jesus
Christ!

The difference between proselytizing and evangelism is
the difference between browbeating and faith-sharing, between coercion and free choice, between demanding an
answer and offering a possibility, between pressure and
compassion, between self-serving labor and self-giving
love *(agape)*. What is needed, therefore, is a listening,
caring stance. If the church wants to be understood, it
must seek to understand. If the church really cares, it will
give without expecting anything in return. That is the
nature of service evangelism.

VII. EVANGELISM, CHRISTIAN NURTURE, AND CHURCH RENEWAL

There is one more twofold relationship that needs to be
clarified, that of evangelism to Christian nurture and
church renewal. Both terms deserve much fuller treat-
ment than I shall give them here. Evangelism and Christian nurture have a chronological relationship. Though
they overlap somewhat, evangelism precedes nurture,
which begins with and takes over after the initial commitment is made. Christian nurture is concerned with growth
in faith and understanding, with the Christian life and
service. It is a lifelong process and the church's continuing
responsibility to all its members, from the Cradle Roll to
the Third Age Club.

Evangelism refers to the church's responsibility to the
unchurched in its parish area. It includes sowing the seed

and cultivating the soil of the unsaved. Its concern is the unchurched, the nonbeliever, the "outsider." It, too, is a continuing responsibility, not a crash program that a church tries for a time. It is the nature of the church to be evangelistic. If it is not, it is abrogating its Christian responsibility. Evangelism is at the heart of the church's mission. It is not only something the church does; it represents something the church *is*.

The evangelistic function also includes the process of preparing people for membership and assimilating them into the life of the church. This is the beginning of their Christian nurture and is extremely important in helping to shape the quality of their discipleship. The assimilation process begins with the membership preparation classes and continues through the Service of Reception and the Public Recognition Service, and until the new members have become *meaningfully* involved in the life and work of the church. Assimilation requires follow-through!

The importance of the membership classes cannot be overstressed. Different churches have different ways of preparing people for membership, but regardless of the format there should be some consistent and thorough program for those who are exploring the possibility of joining the church. It should be at least a five- or six-week experience, conducted by the pastor himself. I see it as an opportunity for team-building, a chance to get to know the people as friends, even before they join, and for them to get to know their pastor. For those attending the classes it is relational, educational, inspirational, and motivational. It is a chance to explore their own faith with other seekers, perhaps at a deeper level than ever before. It affords them the opportunity to ask any questions, raise any concerns, express any doubts, share any ideas, or consider any barriers to faith *before* they join the church. The purpose is to enable them to take their membership vows with integrity, and if they find they cannot, then they should not join.

For me the membership classes are one of the most

satisfying phases of my ministry, climaxed by a very meaningful Service of Reception on the fifth night, during
which each candidate makes a personal statement of faith.
After a brief worship service, during which there are usually some to be baptized or received on confession of faith
and the laying on of hands, there is a time of fellowship
and refreshment. The Public Recognition Service takes
place the following Sunday, when the entire congregation
has an opportunity to meet and to greet the newest members of our church family.

The assimilation process can be greatly facilitated by
some sort of sponsor system. For several years at Second
Presbyterian Church we have followed a practice of assigning an elder to each new candidate for membership.
A written set of instructions is given to each elder, spelling
out his or her duties before, during, and after the Service
of Reception. Included is a description of the examination
process with suggested questions to stimulate a faith-sharing experience and a serious discussion of the meaning of
the membership vows. (See Appendix A.) After having
attended the inquirers classes the candidates are ready for
such an interview, and they bring with them that night
their stewardship commitment cards as a tangible expression of their commitment to Christ and the church.

Because of the number of new members being received
and the many other demands on their time as elders, we
are now enlisting other church members in the assimilation process. As soon as Mr. and Mrs. Jones have expressed
interest in joining the church, a sponsor is assigned, whose
responsibility it is to befriend and shepherd them during
their first year as members. The sponsor's duties include
accompanying their candidates to and being present for
the Service of Reception, accompanying them to and sitting with them at the Public Recognition Service, escort-
ing them to the Fellowship Hour following the service,
introducing them to other members of the congregation
and to appropriate church organizations, accompanying

them to the Annual Congregational Meeting and other church affairs, noting whether or not they are in church, and being aware of and concerned for their general welfare.

Those who are serving as sponsors are instructed as to the importance of their role and the duties required of them. They are an essential part of the assimilation process and the best way to prevent a new member from becoming an early backslider. To be sure, not all sponsors are fulfilling their role as they should. Some are more conscientious and more effective than others. But a pastor who institutes such a system will in time produce a corps of people who see this as their special service to the church, just as others will recognize that their unique calling is to be sowers of the seed. Both functions are necessary parts of any effective evangelism program.

The term "church renewal" refers to the conscious effort to rejuvenate a church's program and revitalize the faith of its people. The need for renewal is due to the fact that our efforts to assimilate often fail, and that our successes are not always lasting. Most people, when they join a church, are sincere in their intentions to be faithful members. But there are always some who fail to live up to their membership vows. Church renewal is aimed at the "backslider" or peripheral member, who has fallen away from the church or ceased to be active. The style of interpersonal witnessing advocated in Chapter 6 is appropriate for calling on backsliding members as well as on unchurched strangers. Most of the principles described would apply in either case.

The membership committee or whatever committee of the church is charged with the pastoral oversight of the congregation should be involved in a persistent program to "win back" inactive members. It, too, is a continuing responsibility and one that is vital to the spiritual life of the church.

Church renewal, however, can actually be a barrier to

or an escape from the church's responsibility to cultivate new members, i.e., evangelism! How often I have heard the comment, "We have to get our own house in order before we start reaching out to others." The trouble is that they never get their own house in order, and hence they never reach out to others! Thus the need for church renewal becomes an excuse for not doing evangelism, which should be directed to the outsider, not the insider.

It sounds plausible to say we ought to reactivate our own members first. But why not do both? Besides, the best way to renew the church is to start reaching out to others! When the church begins to think about the people "out there," more people "in here" will be turned on.

Backsliders, like the poor, we will always have with us. But Jesus' comment was not intended as an excuse for doing nothing. He did not mean we should accept poverty as a proper condition of life, nor should we accept inactivity and absenteeism as an acceptable quality of churchmanship. Church renewal, therefore, will always be a legitimate emphasis.

But once again, it is not an either/or but a both/and relationship. Church renewal will take place much more surely when a church becomes evangelistic, as it will if the church really cares for people—all people.

5

An Evangelistic Style

The apostle Paul certainly did care for people!

Those who wish to engage in service evangelism, as I have defined and described it in the preceding chapter, would do well to study the evangelistic style of the man from Tarsus. From Paul's example we can see that there is a time for proclamation, a time for teaching, and a time for witnessing. We see Paul as the proclaimer in the synagogue at Antioch of Pisidia (Acts 13), in the synagogues at Thessalonica and Beroea (Acts 17), in the Areopagus at Athens (Acts 17), and in the synagogue at Ephesus (Acts 19). We see him as the teacher in the upper room at Troas, where he spoke so long that Eutychus went to sleep and fell out of the window (Acts 20)! Paul's letters are full of teaching.

Then again we see Paul bearing witness on the steps of the Roman barracks in Jerusalem (Acts 22), before Felix the governor (Acts 24), and before Festus and Agrippa (Acts 26). It is interesting that Paul witnessed to outsiders such as Felix, Festus, and Agrippa. He spoke with authority about a Lord and Savior he knew personally. He shared himself, his own experience, and it was powerful!

We get a feeling for Paul's style, as we hear him addressing his audience in the Areopagus, for example: "Men of Athens, I perceive that in every way you are very religious" (Acts 17:22). Paul identified with his hearers where they were and moved on from there. "What therefore you worship as unknown, this I proclaim to you" (Acts 17:23). Paul's was a positive approach, but that did not guarantee him a favorable response in Athens, where he was mocked by some, when they heard about the resurrection.

I. AMBASSADORS FOR CHRIST

Paul called himself an ambassador for Christ. In diplomatic terms an ambassador is someone who is commissioned to speak on behalf of his government. As Christians we, too, are called to speak and act on behalf of our Lord Jesus Christ. What are the requirements? One must first of all be *vocal,* which means being willing to express oneself. "God was in Christ reconciling the world to himself . . . and entrusting to us the message of reconciliation. So we are ambassadors for Christ," said Paul, "God making his appeal through us" (II Cor. 5:19–20). Christ's ambassadors must be ready, willing, and able to speak in his behalf.

But how many of us are? For years the various denominations have been stressing the importance and urgency of evangelism. Pronouncement after pronouncement has charged churches to accept their evangelistic responsibility and to make it a top priority in their ministry. But few churches are fulfilling that obligation, and within those congregations which are attempting to do so the task has usually been relegated to a handful of people.

We shall never fulfill the Great Commission until we realize that evangelism is everybody's job. That does not mean that everyone should be a Billy Graham. It does mean that everyone should be part of the evangelistic enterprise. When you invite a friend to church, or welcome a stranger after a worship service, or talk to a child about Jesus, or comfort a grieving neighbor, or visit a lonely shut-in who has no church home, or tell a backsliding friend you miss seeing her in church, or do anything that communicates the love of Jesus Christ to someone who needs his love but may not know him personally, you are an evangelist of sorts.

In addition to being vocal, an ambassador is also *vulnerable*, which means being willing to expose oneself. "Our mouth is open to you, Corinthians; our heart is wide," said Paul (II Cor. 6:11). He had no secrets from them. His life was an open book. They knew his weaknesses, his humanity, his innermost feelings. He abased himself so that they might be exalted, and he boasted of his weaknesses in order that they might know that his strength was in Christ, not in himself.

But when one is that honest, one can be deeply hurt. One's feelings can be misunderstood, one's motives misjudged, one's words misinterpreted, one's cause misrepresented, one's integrity impugned, one's intelligence questioned, one's intentions suspected, one's confidences betrayed. Paul poured out his heart to Festus and Agrippa, and what was their reaction? "Paul, you are mad." When he proclaimed Christ to the Greeks, the Judaizers said he was acting against the decrees of Caesar.

To be an ambassador for Christ is to be willing to suffer the opposition of those whose toes are stepped on when the gospel is proclaimed. The first effect of our Christian witness may not be reconciliation but alienation, not peace but a sword, not confession but conflict. That is the risk we must take, for our calling is to be God's agents of reconciliation in such a world. So Paul could say, "We are treated as impostors, and yet are true; as unknown, and yet well known; as dying, and behold we live; as punished, and yet not killed; as sorrowful, yet always rejoicing; as poor, yet making many rich; as having nothing, and yet possessing everything" (II Cor. 6:8–10).

An ambassador, then, must be willing to be vulnerable, as well as vocal. And finally, an ambassador for Christ must be *available,* which means being willing to expend oneself. "I will most gladly spend and be spent for your souls," said Paul (II Cor. 12:15). This is what distinguishes service evangelism from the kind of proselytizing described in Chapter 4. Service evangelism is not a hit-and-run relationship. When one encounters a need, one must be concerned to help meet it. That is a commitment to be available, and it means being willing to expend oneself in whatever way is called for by the situation.

When we minister to the needs of people, our ministry will include their material needs, as well as their spiritual needs. At Second Presbyterian Church we are trying to combine in a creative and effective way these two inseparable dimensions of ministry, as we mobilize and utilize the personal and financial resources of the church to serve the needs of the broader community. Our awareness of those needs has been heightened and sensitized by the outreach of those who have been serving as Ambassadors for Christ in our visitation program. As they call in the homes of our neighbors, our callers reflect the love of a church that really cares, and that is expressing that love in tangible ways. Many of the people to whom we have ministered and are ministering will never join our church, but they know we care.

Many do join, however, and that is one of the exciting benefits of such a program. Some people reject evangelism because they see it solely as an activity to bring people into the church. "You're playing the numbers game," they say. Such a comment always raises a red flag for me. What is wrong with bringing people into the church? The book of Numbers may not be the most important book of the Bible, but neither is the book of Exodus! As George Sweazey has commented, "It does not sound as if Luke was unhappy when he wrote in the book of Acts that three thousand souls were added to the church on the Day of Pentecost." Most church denominations have emphasized forthrightly the need for recruitment. For me there is no valid commitment to Jesus Christ unless it includes a commitment to the church for which Christ gave his life. I speak as a churchman, and without apology.

Nevertheless, the quality of any evangelistic program is not to be measured solely by the statistical gains, for what some churches call evangelism may be sheer prosyletizing. The integrity of service evangelism is the willingness of those involved to be vocal, to be vulnerable, and to be available. That's what it means to be an ambassador for Christ.

II. ALWAYS IN TRIUMPH

It is also what I mean by an incarnational approach, which does involve interpersonal witnessing. Here again we can learn from Paul, who has given us a succinct description of his own evangelistic style in II Cor. 2:14–17. *"Thanks be to God,"* he begins. Note that Paul gives the credit to God right from the start. Let us never for a moment think that it is by our technique, or method, or cleverness that anyone is ultimately won to Christ. You and I are the evangelists, but God is the converter. As his witnesses we are simply the instruments he uses to lead others to himself.

"Thanks be to God, *who in Christ always leads us in triumph.*" What a powerful affirmation of faith! It means that when we are with Christ we are with a winner. Paul uses the metaphor of a triumphant Roman conqueror leading his defeated captives into the city. So Paul sees himself as captive to Jesus Christ, the once-proud Pharisee having surrendered his trust in his own goodness to the Lord who brought him to his knees on the road to Damascus. Just as the parade of prisoners chained to the chariots of war was visible evidence of a Roman hero's victory in battle, so, too, Paul's very bondage was a testimony and tribute to Christ's triumph over him and over the world.

So Paul could exclaim, "Thanks be to God, who in Christ always leads us in triumph, *and through us spreads the fragrance of the knowledge of him everywhere.*" Through us: we are God's agents, his hands, his feet, his mouth. Yes, he uses even the likes of us to make himself known. The reference to a fragrant smell continues the image of the triumphal procession, on which occasions incense was often burned in honor of the conquering hero. But in his characteristic way Paul shifts the image to that of the sacrifice, in which sweet-smelling incense was burned as an offering to God. So, too, the knowledge of Christ is revealed through the lives of those whom he has led captive, and that knowledge for Paul was like the fragrance of incense, because it revealed the sweetness and grace of God's redeeming love.

III. THE AROMA OF CHRIST

"For we are the aroma of Christ to God," says Paul. May it ever be thus—Christ in us, shining in our lives, a sweet-smelling offering to God. As evangelists, as witnesses, "we are the aroma of Christ to God *among those who are being saved and among those who are perishing."* Here is Paul's description of our field of labor. It reminds us that salvation is an ongoing process, not an accomplished fact. It began with the life, death, and resurrection of Jesus Christ, and it will be consummated at the end of time, when Christ will come again and all creation will be redeemed. Salvation, therefore, should be spoken of in the present and future tenses, as well as in the past. We who believe in Jesus Christ can say we have been saved, we are being saved, and we hope to be saved—past, present, future!

We live in the present, of course, and for that reason Paul speaks of two kinds of people, those who are being saved and those who are perishing. At any given point in time everybody is traveling one of two roads: Salvation Street or Hell's Highway. I remember singing years ago a cowboy song that described the road to "that bright happy region" as a dim, narrow trail, while the broad one leading to Hades "is posted and blazed all the way."

The point to which Paul is speaking here is not whether

a person on Hell's Highway can be saved. Rather, Paul is underscoring the truth that how a person responds to the gospel of Christ depends on which road he is traveling at the time. "To those who are perishing," says Paul, *"it is a fragrance from death to death."* That is, to those who are already on the way to spiritual death, the aroma of Christ is offensive, and their rejection of it only speeds them farther along the way to ruin. But to those who are spiritually alive, to those who are open and receptive to the gospel, to those who are seekers after truth, the aroma is *"a fragrance from life to life,"* and thus any encounter with the gospel is another boost toward salvation.

There is a tremendous truth here that has been confirmed over and over again by our Second Church Ambassadors, as they call on people in our neighborhood. Almost everybody has been exposed to enough of God to decide which road to travel. Before we ever ring a doorbell, God has already been there, and our task is to help people to discover and acknowledge that, and to act on it. What a tremendous responsibility! To think that the witness of our words and our lives could be a doorway to death or to life for someone.

IV. NOT PEDDLERS

"Who is sufficient for these things?" asks Paul. If the apostle Paul felt inadequate for the task, how much more should we! But the point is that he didn't feel inadequate. Paul's question implies that he felt the stupendous burden of the evangelistic task, as do we. It would seem that no one is sufficient for such a task, but what follows shows that Paul felt that he was, and we are: *"For we are not, like so many, peddlers of God's word."*

We are sufficient, says Paul, because we are not out hustling for God. We are not trying to merchandise Jesus. We are not a bunch of religious hucksters, peddlers of God's word. The Greek expression means literally "those who adulterate God's word." There were plenty of them around in Paul's day and there are plenty around today. Read the newspaper ads of some churches. You would think we are supposed to sell Christ the way we sell toothpaste. We are called to be witnesses, not salespersons. There is a big difference between selling a product and sharing one's faith. The only one who ever sold Christ, sold him out—for thirty pieces of silver!

"We are not . . . peddlers of God's word; *but as men "*— I'm sure if Paul were writing today he would say as *persons* —*"of sincerity. "* There was nothing phony about Paul. He was a man of integrity, who knew what he believed and why he believed it. I don't think any evangelistic enterprise has validity until the people involved in it have examined their own faith and can say with conviction and with sincerity, "I believe in a personal God, a God who responds to my prayers and to whom I am responsible, a God who has revealed himself to humankind in a man called Jesus of Nazareth."

Any preacher who cannot believe that should get out of the ministry fast! How can one presume to step into a pulpit and preach in the name of Jesus Christ if one cannot confess him as personal Lord and Savior? How can one dare to say "thus says the Lord!" if one does not feel called into his service?

Some have quit the ministry because they feel they can no longer preach with integrity. They have lost their faith in a personal God. They think religious language is meaningless, that no faith statements can be normative, and that people who use God talk are merely playing a religious language game. If they are right, then we are just kidding ourselves: our worship is only so much liturgical nonsense, and our witness is empty rhetoric.

Paul was not playing games, and neither are we. Integrity demands that we know *that* we believe, and *why* we believe, and *what* we believe, *"as commissioned by God. "* Our evangelistic responsibility has been laid upon us by

Christ himself. We are called to be his witnesses. Knowing that, we have no choice. How can anyone claim to be his disciple and refuse to be his witness? The question is not, Should we be evangelists? but, What kind of evangelists are we?

Evangelists who know that God has commissioned them know that God is with them in their labors: "As commissioned by God, *in the sight of God.*" That is, in God's presence, with God's blessing, by God's power, for God's glory, and according to God's wisdom. "In the sight of God *we speak*"—always ready to speak a word, always ready to give a reason for the hope that is within us, always ready, sometimes fearfully willing and, we hope, able to take our stand for Christ, to be counted on the side of truth, to show that we are not ashamed of the gospel of Christ.

"In the sight of God we speak *in Christ*"—in the name of Christ, in the spirit of Christ, in the manner of Christ, and for the sake of Christ. That is Paul's style of evangelism and, we hope, ours as well, as we fulfill our role as ambassadors for Christ and members of his servant church.

6

Interpersonal Witnessing

I. VISITATION EVANGELISM

How does one go about fulfilling the role of ambassador? If a local church exists to serve people—not only its own members but the community in which it is situated—then it must minister to people's needs. To do that, it has to know what their needs are. In order to know what their needs are, its ambassadors have to go where the people are. That is the simplest way I know to justify some kind of evangelistic calling program.

The popular term for such a program is "visitation evangelism," which evokes from many people, unfortunately, a negative reaction, usually because they have failed to make the kinds of distinctions we pointed out in Chapter 4. Some of their concerns are quite legitimate. Too many well-intentioned doorbell ringers in their "zeal for the Lord" have been overly aggressive and totally insensitive to where people are.

This was brought home to me a few years ago when I was visiting a young couple in Florida who were former members of the Oak Lane Presbyterian Church. When I asked them why they had not joined a nearby Presbyterian church, they explained that they had been completely turned off by those who had visited them from the congregation. "They made us feel as if we weren't Christians, and we resented it. That church puts too much pressure on people."

The thought of "ringing doorbells for Christ" elicited an angry response from one member of an evangelism committee for whom I had been invited to conduct a workshop in a Baltimore church. "Our congregation is much too sophisticated for that sort of thing," she declared. "Why, just the other day two religious fanatics came to my door and I made the mistake of inviting them in. They stayed, and they stayed, and they stayed, and they were obnoxious." Other heads were nodding in agreement.

"You remind me," I said, "of the story of the man who had a pet flea, which he trained to jump at his command. He decided to conduct an experiment to see what would happen if he cut off two of the flea's legs. The flea still jumped at his command, but with some difficulty. So he cut off two more of the flea's legs, and the flea still managed to jump, but with much greater difficulty. Finally he cut off the remaining legs, and this time when he said jump, the flea didn't jump. He shouted louder, and the flea still didn't jump. So he wrote down the conclusion of his experiment: when you cut off a flea's legs it becomes deaf and can no longer hear your commands!"

The woman had the right facts but drew the wrong conclusion. The peril of non sequiturs! So she was called on by two persons who were obnoxious. Therefore, what? Don't call? No, therefore don't be obnoxious! There is a way to do evangelistic calling that is not at all objectionable. It is not the purpose of this book to develop a case for visitation evangelism. That I have already tried to do in *The Oak Lane Story,* which is the case study of a church that took seriously its responsibility to be a servant community. For now, I am assuming that a visitation program of some kind needs no justification. But *what* kind? *That* we should call is for me a given; *how* we should call is what needs to be determined.

As I stated in Chapter 4, the purpose of P.R.O.O.F. is to

help people to become more effective ambassadors for Christ. Service evangelism calls for a special style of interpersonal witnessing which I have described as incarnational rather than propositional. In this chapter I shall try to elaborate on that distinction.

II. SERVICE EVANGELISM

The main thing to remember in service evangelism is that the initial purpose in calling on people is what the name implies: service. The callers are there to listen, to empathize, to show they care, to be friends. Behind every door there is a need of some kind, and sensitive callers will usually discover it. As tactfully as possible and without being pushy, they hope to communicate their desire and their availability to be helpful. This is the agenda, and it is quite different from the aggressive approach that so offended my Florida friends. They didn't want to be browbeaten into a "decision for Christ."

Service evangelism is more than what has been popularly called "friendship evangelism," which as it is generally practiced is not need-oriented and requires little or no follow-through. Ambassadors for Christ, as we have said, must be willing to be available as a need arises. If they themselves cannot meet the need, they enlist whatever help is available from the church.

So when the callers discover an elderly widow who is living alone and apparently unable to care for herself, they will endeavor to discover what kind of help is needed. Is it financial assistance? Is it a friend, someone to visit her? Is it someone to do her marketing, take her to the doctor, do her errands? Perhaps she needs to be in a nursing home but has no one, no way, and no incentive to explore that possibility. Whatever the need, she becomes an object of the callers' pastoral concern, and they report the information to the pastor, to the board of deacons, or to whatever committee or person in the church is responsible for the ministry of compassion.

Or maybe it is a young man recently released from prison, with no job, no friends, no hope. The church can become for him a supportive, caring community, where he can find acceptance and encouragement as well as help in looking for a job, and in the process regain his self-respect and feeling of self-worth.

Or maybe it is a family who are feeling the aloofness or even the hostility of some of their neighbors, and who would deeply appreciate the callers' warm and sincere desire to welcome them into the fellowship of the church.

It is obvious that the callers cannot meet every need they encounter. Their responsibility is to enlist the total resources of the church in the ministry of compassion, ideally with the entire congregation involved in some way or another, if only vicariously. That ideal may never be attained, but the closer a congregation comes to it, the more helpful and productive its ministry will be and the greater the impact it will have on the spiritual growth of its own members.

III. Service EVANGELISM

The initial purpose, then, is service. But that is not the only purpose. We are not mere social workers. We are ambassadors for Christ. Our Christian witness is not a hidden agenda. To pretend otherwise would be not only hypocritical but a betrayal of our calling. The point is not *whether* to witness for Christ, but when and how to witness. That is where some skill is needed, and why training is necessary. At Second Church our Ambassadors (who call for the church on Monday nights) must have attended a P.R.O.O.F. seminar before they can take part in the calling program. Assuming you have had that training, which includes several hours of role-playing typical calling situations, what do you say when you ring the doorbell?

IV. The Approach

Let us assume that you are calling on persons of whom you have no previous knowledge, as is usually the case when you are engaged in a door-to-door program of visitation evangelism. It is important always to remember that *the call begins before you ever ring the doorbell.* It begins as you and your partner have a brief prayer together before you get out of the car, or before you walk up to the front door. It is a simple prayer for God's presence with you and the persons upon whom you are calling, that the Holy Spirit will prepare the way and make it a meaningful visit for everyone.

What you say when the doorbell is answered is extremely important and the only structured part of the call. That is one of the major differences between this approach and James Kennedy's "evangelism explosion" or Campus Crusade's Four Spiritual Laws, which are highly structured and propositional. The hope is that you will be invited into the home for a brief visit. Your opening statement is intended to enable that to happen. It must accomplish five things:

1. *Identify* who you are: "We're from Community Methodist Church,

2. *Explain* why you are there: and we're calling on our neighbors.

3. *Acknowledge* the intrusion: We hope this is not an inconvenient time,

4. *Ask* to come in: but we would love to visit with you

5. *Promise* to be brief: for just a moment."

Our Ambassadors have found that this approach works very well, but they are free to modify it or use an entirely

different one, so long as it works. The test is whether they
are getting into the homes! If the call is on persons who
have had a previous contact with the church (someone
who has signed the guest book, for example), our Ambassadors will usually be invited into the home. If they are not,
they ask when it would be convenient to call again, and,
if possible, they make a date for the next regular calling
night. If that time is not suitable, they set a date that is
mutually convenient.

If it is what we call a "probe" call, where there has been
no previous contact, the visit may take place on the doorstep. In that case the call becomes more of a "census." All
the caller can hope to do is to obtain some basic information about the family, including their religious affiliation,
if any; ask if there is any way the church can be of service;
and invite them to a worship service. If they are unchurched, a follow-up call is in order, and this is noted on
the card.

I learned years ago that it is impractical to try to set up
calling appointments in advance, unless you want to make
sure someone is home and can see you, to avoid your
making a long trip to no avail. Otherwise it is far better to
give the calling teams enough cards in the same general
area and let them take their chances on finding a certain
percentage of the people home. Our contact percentage
at Second Presbyterian Church is running close to seventy
percent!

The fact that the callers have not made an appointment
makes it all the more important that they acknowledge
the intrusion right at the start, and assure the people upon
whom they are calling that they won't stay more than a
few minutes. One reason some families are reluctant to
invite church callers in is that they are afraid the callers
may stay too long. Put them at ease on that point immediately!

V. Inside the Home

Once you get into the home you play it by ear, literally and figuratively—literally because you are there to listen, figuratively because you are not there to give a memorized "spiel." How you respond and what you say depend entirely upon the situation, and every situation is different. You rely on the Holy Spirit to prompt you when to speak and when not to speak, and to put the right words in your mouth.

It has been agreed in advance that one of the two callers will take the lead and the other will be the supportive, but not a silent, partner. At no time will the callers allow themselves to be drawn into separate conversations with the persons they are visiting, and they will try to place themselves so that the two of them will be facing the person or persons they are visiting. It is very disconcerting to have to play verbal ping-pong while trying to carry on a conversation. In my own calling, if I see that the seating arrangement is not working out properly, I do not hesitate to ask if I may take another seat or move my chair "so I can look at both of you."

Many inexperienced callers allow themselves to be seated in a manner that invites what I call "cross-firing," "sidetracking," or "yoo-hooing." Cross-firing occurs when the callers are on opposite sides of the other person and hence coming at him from two different directions:

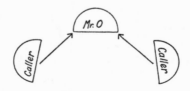

Sidetracking occurs when each caller engages in a separate conversation with the closest person, as indicated:

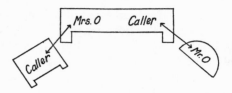

Yoo-hooing is what happens when the persons are seated so far apart that they feel as if they are shouting at one another across the room. In a situation like that I ask the hostess if she would mind if I move a small chair over closer to them so that I can see and hear them better.

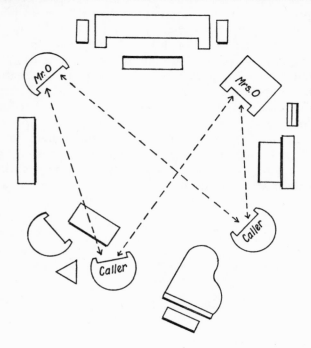

An unfavorable seating arrangement is one of the most frequent handicaps that callers must learn to handle. Another is the television. Never try to compete with a television set; you will lose every time, in one way or another. If the television is on when you enter the room, there are several things you can do. The first thing is to apologize for interrupting their television program. Most persons are gracious enough to turn it off at that point, and if they do, make sure you cut the visit *very* short, unless they *sincerely* want you to stay a little longer. If they turn the sound down but leave the picture on, it is obvious they are more interested in the program than in visiting with you, so offer to come back another time. You might say something like this:

> CALLER: Look, we don't want to interrupt your TV show. We'll come back another time. In the meantime, if there is any way we can be of help to you folks, we sure hope you'll call upon us. May we stop back again?

Many times that will induce them to turn off the set. If not, they will usually be so glad to get rid of you so they can get back to their program that they will eagerly agree to a return visit. In that case, you have paved the way for the next visit.

If they leave both the sound and the picture on, but offer you a seat and seem to be willing to talk, don't try to outshout the television. On the contrary, *lower* your voice. Your host or hostess, in straining to hear, will often automatically get up and turn off the set. If that doesn't happen, there is one last tactic you can try before giving up, assuming they are not trying to watch the program out of the corner of their eye:

> CALLER: Would you mind my turning off the television? I'm having trouble concentrating on what you're saying . . . unless you're watching it?

If that doesn't work, you may as well leave, for you are obviously an intruder, not a guest.

Television is only one of the many distractions that can occur in a home. It may be a capering canine that is either too friendly and insists on leaping all over you, or not friendly enough and drowns out your doorstep conversation with its angry yelping. Or it may be a young child, whose constant interruptions make conversation impossible. Or it may be an unexpected visit from a neighbor, whose presence changes the agenda completely. Any of these things can be an obstacle to communication and prevent a faith-sharing experience. The wise caller must be sensitive and flexible enough to respond to any and all circumstances, and to be ready to make a graceful exit if the circumstances are not right for a visit.

What if one of the spouses stays in another room? The way you handle that situation depends upon how the conversation goes with the one with whom you are talking. If Mrs. O is friendly and receptive, you might ask her at some point:

CALLER: Is your husband not interested in the church?

MRS. O: Not the least.

CALLER: Is that why he stayed out in the kitchen?

MRS. O: Yes, he doesn't want to be pressured into going to church.

CALLER: We certainly don't intend to do that. But we would at least like to say hello. Do you think he would be willing to do that?

MRS. O: I don't know. I'll see if he'll come in and say hello.

It is important for the callers to establish a relationship with Mr. O if at all possible. He has to make his own decision about church, and the callers, by relating only to his wife, could be driving the wedge between him and his wife (regarding their church relationship) even deeper. It is far better, if at all possible, to visit with both of them at once. If that is not possible, the callers should make it a point to come back again for the express purpose of visiting with Mr. O.

Assuming the situation is favorable for a visit, how do you start? Although you as the caller do not have a set "plan of attack" as you would in what I have called the propositional approach to evangelism, you need a way to begin, and it is always best to begin by getting acquainted. If you are a caring person and a good listener, you will have no difficulty getting them to talk about themselves. Using a nondirective approach and with good leading questions, you will be amazed at how quickly even strangers will open up. As they do, you will be sensitive for hints of need or concern, and for opportunities to offer your services or those of the church. Remember: you are there to be a friend, to make yourself available.

But an Ambassador is also ready, willing, and able to be vocal, and you will therefore be looking for opportunities to share your faith. It is better by far if these opportunities can develop naturally out of the conversation. For example, a widow has been telling you about the recent death of her husband and how her faith has helped her through that crisis. Your nondirective response: "You say your faith in God has helped you. . . ." Invariably the person will then elaborate, and it is a faith-sharing situation.

Sometimes you have to make your own opportunity for faith-sharing. After hearing a sad tale: "What part does your faith play in all this?" Or even more direct: "You say you have never belonged to a church; do you believe in God?" And then, "How do you feel about Jesus Christ?" The object is to get the other person to share her faith. The caller should be more eager to listen than to speak.

VI. SOME THOUGHTS ABOUT LISTENING

But how to listen?

I remember a "Grin and Bear It" cartoon that expressed one of the world's great needs. It showed two rather corpulent women in the waiting room of a doctor's office. One was saying to the other: "It's agreed, Adele! We'll trade symptoms and find out if he really listens."

There always has been and there always will be a need for listening. So great is the need that we are willing to pay handsome sums to analysts, counselors, and other professionals for listening to us. In Taylor Caldwell's book *The Listener* (Doubleday & Co., 1960), wise old John Godfrey expresses a universal lament when he tells a reporter, "Nobody really listens" (p. 21).

Why don't we listen? For one thing, we're too busy. We have no time for listening. Everyone is preoccupied. Our minds are filled with our own thoughts, our own needs, our own worries and problems. "Don't tell me your troubles, I've got troubles of my own." That's the story with all of us. We're too busy, too busy talking to listen.

Not only are we too busy to listen, we don't know how to listen. In recognition of this fact many books are being written by educators, psychologists, and the like, on the art of listening. What a tragedy that we have to speak of listening as an art!

Recognizing this need, some churches have formed structured listening groups to give people the opportunity to be listened to and to listen. In the P.R.O.O.F. seminars we spend a considerable amount of time learning to listen. If one wishes to be a good witness for Christ, *one must first know how to listen.*

Another problem is that we think much faster than we talk. While the average American speaks at the rate of about 125 words a minute, ideas race through the brain at much higher speeds. This means that our brains can re-

ceive the spoken words and still have spare time for thinking. We go on mental sidetracks, and thus miss part of
what the speaker is saying. We also tend to memorize
facts, instead of listening for ideas, and this, too, hampers
our listening ability.

Still another deterrent to good listening is our tendency
to employ emotional filters, in the hearing process. We
listen attentively to what we want to hear, while shutting
out that which we do not. Too often our critical faculties
are crippled by our emotional involvement. When someone hits upon one of our pet peeves or prejudices, we stop
listening and begin rehearsing all of our objections, without hearing the other person out. Every preacher and
teacher is familiar with this pattern of behavior.

All of this points up the fact that we don't know how to
listen. And yet, God wants us to listen. He has given us this
highly sensitive and delicately specialized instrument we
call an ear. But how we waste it! We don't listen to our
fellow human beings, and we don't listen to God. When I
don't listen to my brother, I fail myself, because I shut off
my chance to learn. I fail my brother, because I don't
understand him, and when I don't understand him, I can't
help him.

The president of our junior class at seminary was a
handsome young man, big and strong, with an athletic
build, and intelligent—a Phi Beta Kappa at Dartmouth.
Yet Dick seemed to be worried about something. His
roommate noticed it. His friends in the dormitory noticed it. But they passed over it. All of us were busy
with our studies. The pressure was terrific. Finally, the
school year ended, we said good-by to one another for
the summer. When we returned in the fall we heard
the news. Dick had committed suicide. Perhaps if
someone had listened . . .

When I don't listen, I also fail God, for it is he who has
given us the capacity to listen. We forfeit that right when
we are too busy, too distracted, too preoccupied to hear

what the other person is saying. God wants us to listen to one another. And he wants us to listen to him. "O that my people would listen to me!" (Ps. 81:13). The Old Testament prophets cried out in despair at Israel's refusal to listen to the word of God. "For twenty-three years . . . the word of the Lord has come to me," said Jeremiah, "and I have spoken persistently to you, but you have not listened" (Jer. 25:3). "O that you had hearkened to my commandments!" spoke Isaiah in the name of the Lord (Isa. 48:18).

"He who has ears to hear, let him hear," declared Jesus in the New Testament (Matt. 11:15). "This is my beloved Son, with whom I am well pleased," said the voice of God on the Mount of Transfiguration; "listen to him" (Matt. 17:5).

Given the importance of listening, how do you teach someone the art of listening? Educators think they can teach children to improve their listening ability. But I am not sure people can be *taught* to listen caringly. Can you teach people to care? Can you teach people to love? What is needed is sensitivity training—not the kind we usually hear about. I am talking about an ability to relate to other people, a spiritual empathy, a genuine interest in and compassion for others. Such a quality is a gift of God. Can you teach something that is a gift? I don't know the answer to that question. But I do think you can help people to see what it means to listen.

You may not be able to teach someone to love, but you can show someone what love requires. You may not be able to teach a person to care, but you can help a person to see what a caring person does. You may not be able to teach someone to listen, but you can help someone to understand what it means to be a good listener. To that end I offer the C Rules of Good Listening, which the P.R.O.O.F. seminar participants discuss and try to apply as they role-play various situations.

COMPASSION

The word "compassion" literally means "to suffer with," from the Latin *com* ("with") and *pati* ("suffer"). To listen well, I must love sincerely; to love sincerely, I must have a genuine compassion for others. I must be able to feel what the other person feels, to share his or her agony, to empathize. That means relating to the other person as an individual, a unique person, not a "type" to be classified and labeled.

CONCENTRATION

The other person must feel that I am really "hearing" him or her, really listening. That means focusing my attention, my eyes as well as my ears on the person, concentrating on what is being said and not what I want to say next. It means learning to read expressions and "body language," so that I discern the feelings behind the words. It also means that my own facial expressions and body language must convey to the other person that my complete attention is assured. Face language, like all other forms of communication, is a two-way process.

CONTROL

I must learn when to speak and when not to speak. I must control my urge to answer every question asked, or to say more than I need to say. I must not be threatened by silence, realizing that I need not fill every gap with words. That takes patience and sensitivity—self-control!

COMPREHENSION

I must try to understand where the other person is "coming from." My responsibility as a listener is not to agree, but to comprehend. I must remember that how we relate to each other is always affected by our previous experiences. I need not be threatened, therefore, by the other person's negative reaction to me, nor should

I stop listening when my own reaction is negative. I
must comprehend "what's going on" as well as what's
being said!

CLARIFICATION

Clarification is an essential part of good listening. It
assumes and depends upon comprehension. If I myself
understand what's going on, I can help the other person
to discover it as well, by raising questions that help to
clarify the issues or decision being faced. A good listener
helps the other person to understand the situation being
described.

COMMITMENT

Good listening presupposes a relationship, and as a
Christian I am committed to do what love demands. If
I am genuinely concerned for the other person, then I
must make myself available. I give the lie to my listening
if I don't follow through in whatever way is called for.
In other words, good listening must issue in appropriate
action.

There is nothing definitive or exhaustive about these
rules. All of us have our own ideas about listening. These
are my own attempt to identify some basic ingredients of
the art of listening in an effort to stimulate some self-
examination on the part of the P.R.O.O.F. seminar participants. I must admit that in spite of the emphasis on
helping people to understand the importance of listening
and to develop their own listening skills, some people
never seem to become good listeners, and consequently
they do not make good ambassadors for Christ. It is not
that they are unwilling or unable to share their own
faith. It is their inability to allow others to share theirs. It
is no solution to the problem to say that the art of listening is a gift of God, but it helps if the seminar leader
recognizes and understands the problem. All the leader

can hope to do is help people to develop their own God-
given capacity to listen. That's all, but that is extremely
important, for good listening is an indispensable ingredi-
ent of service evangelism.

VII. SOME THOUGHTS ABOUT SPEAKING

But so is speaking. So the next question is, What do you
say when you do speak? You share your own faith, not the
reasons you think the other person should believe, but the
reasons *you* believe; not the conversion experience you
had twenty years ago, but the recent evidences of God in
your life. In other words, what has he done for you lately?
You can't share a faith if you don't have a faith to share!
You should be able to speak with sincerity, conviction, and
authority on your own experience.

But don't monopolize the conversation. You don't have
to tell it all at once. Wait for the right moment, and when
you speak, clothe your responses in your own experience.
Speak from the heart, not from the head. Feel sincerely
what you say, or don't say it. Let the person know how you
feel, not what you think. Most important, lead from weak-
ness, not from strength. Identify with the other person in
his or her struggle, pain, doubt. To do that is to make
yourself vulnerable, but as we have said, as an ambassador
you must be willing to expose yourself.

Part of that exposure is your own fallibility. You don't
have to, nor should you, pose as an authority on all religious questions. We pastors should relieve our people of
that persistent fear of their own ignorance, which is the
major cause of their reluctance to witness. They are well
aware of their own Biblical and theological incompetence.
One of the most helpful and encouraging discoveries they
should make in the P.R.O.O.F. seminar is that they don't
have to be "experts" to be witnesses. They don't have to
answer every question asked. What a tremendous burden

it is to think one has to know everything! What a relief to
be able to say, "I don't know."

So when Mr. Jones asks a pointed question for which
there is no easy answer, the caller can simply say:

CALLER: That's a tough one. I wish I had an answer
for that. What do you think about it?

(Or)
I've often wondered about that myself.

Then wait for the other person to go on, for more often
than not he really does not want to know what you think,
but rather wants to get something off his own chest.

That is not always his motive, of course, for sometimes
a person is indeed searching for answers. In that case the
caller might respond with:

CALLER: That sounds like a theological question to
me. I'll ask my pastor about it and let you know what
he says.

The added benefit of this kind of reply is that it gives the
caller a reason for coming back and opens the way for a
continuing relationship. But don't make any promises you
don't intend to keep! Availability means follow-through!
That's the test of a genuine concern for people.

Such an approach also provides an excellent opportunity for a positive affirmation of the church. For example:

CALLER: I don't know the answer to that question, but
I'm sure my pastor can help me. I'm so grateful to be
part of a church family where this kind of help is
available. I couldn't make it on my own.

(Or)
We've been wrestling with that in our Adult Bible
Class. It's really great to have a group of Christian
friends with whom to discuss these things. We help
each other grow in our faith and understanding.

Would you like to join us next Sunday morning? I'll be happy to stop by for you.

What if you do know the answer? Don't be too eager to say it! A good witness, like a good teacher, tries to enable the other person to discover the truth. A nondirective approach will help that to happen. Let me illustrate by showing two possible responses, one right and one wrong, to the same comment:

MR. JONES: I don't see how you can believe in a God who would let an innocent child be stricken with leukemia.

CALLER: *(wrong response)* Suffering and tragedy of all kinds are always a test of faith. No one can fully understand why these things happen, why the good suffer and the wicked seem to prosper. That's the problem which The Book of Job wrestles with and at the end there is no human answer to the why of suffering. After Job and his friends have tried to explain why Job has undergone all his misery, God says, "Who is this that darkens counsel by words without knowledge? . . . Where were you when I laid the foundation of the earth?"

CALLER: *(right response)* You can't believe in a God who would let a child suffer. . . .

The first response is not really what Mr. Jones wanted to hear. He has something he wants to get off his chest, and the best thing the caller can do is let him express himself. The caller gave a correct answer, but a wrong response. The second response, on the other hand, is no answer at all, but it frees Mr. Jones to continue with his thought. Perhaps Mr. Jones will move from the head level to the heart level, for what he is really concerned about is not the intellectual problem of suffering, but the fact that his own little girl has leukemia.

Now let's assume a situation in which the callers discover that Mrs. Johnson has recently lost her husband. In the course of the visit she opens up to the callers and expresses her great grief. Mrs. Smith, one of the callers, has been through the experience, her husband having died of a heart attack a year ago. She can empathize with Mrs. Johnson, but she should not share that information immediately. To do so is a kind of "griefmanship" which can stifle any further desire on Mrs. Johnson's part to talk about her own grief. "Why should Mrs. Smith want to listen to me? She has her own grief to bear."

It would be far better for Mrs. Smith to wait, perhaps, until just before the callers are ready to leave. Then she might say something like this:

> CALLER: I appreciate your telling us about your husband. He must have been a wonderful man. I know how hard it is to lose someone you love, because I lost my husband a year ago, and I haven't gotten over it yet. But I'm learning to live with it, and I pray that God will help you to live with it, too.

Mrs. Smith has shown Mrs. Johnson that she understands, because she too has experienced grief, but by using restraint in sharing her own loss, Mrs. Smith has also shown Mrs. Johnson that she has really listened to her. How much more meaningful it is to wait. As a caller your aim is to make the other person feel that you have listened, that you have heard her, that you respect her feelings, and that you affirm her as a person.

VIII. SOME THOUGHTS ABOUT USING THE BIBLE

The style of interpersonal witnessing taught in the P.R.O.O.F. model does not depend upon a memorized presentation of the gospel punctuated by selected Scripture passages. That does not mean, however, that the approach is not Biblical, or that the gospel is unimportant, or that the Bible is not to be used. Great pains were taken in Chapter 2 to establish a Biblical and theological rationale for a faith-sharing approach. Once a person understands the givenness of his faith, the Bible then becomes for him the most powerful and persuasive confirmation of faith experience and the authoritative basis for beliefs. He will spend the rest of his life studying the Bible and applying its truths to every dimension of life. The more he knows about the Bible and the more familiar with Scripture he becomes, the more confident and effective he will be in using his Biblical knowledge.

But the P.R.O.O.F. approach is not to use the Bible as a hammer. You can't quote people into the kingdom. First you have to establish a basis for its authority, or at least for its reasonableness, if the other person claims to be an un-believer. If he has not accepted its authority, what good does it do to hurl Scripture quotations at him? If he has accepted the authority of the Bible, then you can use it to help clarify or reinforce a point.

How you use the Bible, then, depends upon the person to whom you are witnessing. If you are not sure where she stands, you might say to the person who has been stating her beliefs or values something like this:

CALLER: How do you arrive at your values? What's the basis of your authority?

MRS. A: My own philosophy of life.

CALLER: How do you feel about the Bible?

MRS. A: I don't believe everything in the Bible.

CALLER: You don't believe everything in the Bi-ble . . .

MRS. A: Not those stories about Adam and Eve, and Jonah and the whale, and that sort of thing. Do you believe all that stuff?

CALLER: I believe the Bible stories give spiritual truth. The Bible is a religious book, not a scientific textbook. It contains many different kinds of literature. Not everything is meant to be taken literally, but the spiritual truths which the stories teach about God and about our relationship to God are as relevant today as they were when they were written. Would you agree with that?

The above conversation assumes a give-and-take discussion in which the caller is sharing his own views rather than using a nondirective approach. If Mrs. A acknowledges that the Bible is indeed a source of truth, then the caller can feel free to cite Scripture passages to document his ideas.

To an unbeliever he might say at some point: "The Bible has something to say about that," and then try to show with appropriate Scripture references how the Biblical insights apply to the topic being discussed. Thus the caller uses the Bible as his authority, not to pound home but to illustrate a point, not as a club to command obedience but as a treasury of inspired truth to illustrate and emphasize and clarify and enlighten.

But that requires knowledge of the Bible!—greater knowledge than a few memorized proof texts. It requires some theological maturity as well. The evangelistic approaches of some fundamentalist groups cannot be faulted on their Biblical emphasis; it is their theology that leaves something to be desired.

I am greatly impressed by the organization and thoroughness of James Kennedy's *Evangelism Explosion* (Tyndale House Publishers, 1970). The theological presuppositions implied in his two introductory questions, however, are incompatible with the principles of P.R.O.O.F.: "If you were to die tonight, where would you spend eternity?" and "If God were to ask you why he should let you into heaven, what would you say?" The questions are intended to open the way for the caller to present the gospel.

So, too, the Four Spiritual Laws of Campus Crusade are a useful tool for those who need a structured way of presenting the gospel to someone who is already comfortable with their language. But notice the undeclared assumption in the very first "law": "God loves you and offers a wonderful plan for your life." That's fine if the other person has already accepted the idea of a personal God. But what if he hasn't? The Four Spiritual Laws assume that the case for God has already been made.

An effective caller is one who is able to relate his knowledge of the Scriptures to whatever question arises. For example:

MR. O: I don't believe in God.

CALLER: What would it take to make you believe in God?

MR. O: For me, seeing is believing.

CALLER: Look, the Bible admits that "no one has ever seen God." That's where Jesus Christ comes in. As John says, "The only Son, who is in the bosom of the Father, he has made him known." If you want to know what God is like, study Jesus.

MR. O: That's another problem for me.

CALLER: You're not the only one. Look how long it took the disciples to get the message. Philip said to Jesus, "Show us the Father, and we shall be satisfied." And Jesus showed his frustration and disappointment when he replied: "Have I been with you so long, and yet you do not know me, Philip? He who has seen me has seen the Father; how can you say 'Show us the Father'?"

MR. O: But they actually lived with him. It's even harder for us.

CALLER: Maybe that's why Jesus said, "Blessed are those who have not seen and yet believe."

MR. O: I wish I could believe.

CALLER: Then you will. Jesus said, "Ask, and it will be given you; seek, and you will find; knock, and it will be opened to you."

MR. O: What if I can't believe, does that mean I won't go to heaven?

CALLER: Heaven is not a place you go to, though we speak of it that way. Heaven is a relationship with God, a personal relationship made known to us, and made possible for us, by Jesus Christ, who said, "I am the way, and the truth, and the life; no one comes to the Father, but by me."

MR. O: What about those who have never heard of Jesus?

CALLER: That isn't for us to decide. God is the Judge of all mankind. But we know that he loves us all. Paul deals with this question in his letter to the Romans, where he makes the point that those who live under the law will be judged according to the law.

MR. O: What did he mean by that?

CALLER: That they would have to earn their salvation by their obedience to the laws of God. But Paul goes on to point out that no one can be saved on that basis, since no one is able to keep the law perfectly.

MR. O: Then who can be saved?

CALLER: Anyone who believes in Jesus Christ. That's the gospel, which means "good news." The good news is that God loves us and accepts us the way we are, and he demonstrated that love in the life, death, and resurrection of Jesus Christ, for as John says, "God so

loved the world that he gave his only Son, that whoever believes in him should not perish but have eternal life."

MR. O: What is eternal life?

CALLER: Jesus said, "This is eternal life, that they
know thee the only true God, and Jesus Christ whom
thou hast sent."

MR. O: So that's what you mean by a personal relationship with God . . .

CALLER: Yes, and it begins the moment one accepts
Jesus Christ as his Lord and Savior. "I write this to you
who believe in the name of the Son of God," said John,
"that you may know that you have eternal life." Present tense! And when one knows God this way, one can
say as Paul said, "I am sure that neither death, nor life,
nor angels, nor principalities, nor things present, nor
things to come, nor powers, nor height, nor depth, nor
anything else in all creation, will be able to separate
us from the love of God in Christ Jesus our Lord."

The purpose of this hypothetical conversation is to show
how the more mature caller uses the Bible. Instead of
delivering a prepared speech, he enters into dialogue with
Mr. O, using Biblical passages as appropriate to illustrate
and authenticate his responses. This assumes that a relationship has been established in which such an intellectual
discussion can comfortably take place, and in which it is
not inappropriate to use a modified (flexible) propositional
approach. The point I wish to make is that the P.R.O.O.F.
approach is not anti-Biblical, but it calls for a different
understanding of *how* and *when* to use the Bible.

IX. SOME THOUGHTS ABOUT WITNESSING

Callers discover what the 1978 Gallup Poll revealed about the religious attitudes of Americans: that most people (7 out of 10) identify themselves as "church members," even though they may not be "working" at it. Some are warm and receptive, although they may not be members of a church. Others are indifferent and unresponsive, and a few are downright hostile, but most people are remarkably friendly and hospitable to those who knock on their doors, if the callers are tactful, sensitive, and sincere.

If a person is a "believer" and willing to talk about his faith, a caller should have no trouble relating and the visit should be a most pleasant and "easy" experience. But let us assume now that the person upon whom you are calling is an outsider, that is, someone who is not identified with a church. What kind of interpersonal witnessing is appropriate?

The first thing to remember is that the agenda is still the same. You are there to listen, to relate, to be available. It never ceases to be *service* evangelism, no matter upon whom you are calling.

But the way you witness will be different. Here it is helpful to recognize what type of outsider you are dealing with. Although I resent and resist labels, I have found that the persons we normally think of as outsiders usually identify themselves as one of three basic types. They may call themselves atheists, or agnostics, or adherents of some other faith. I call this the Type Trio. The atheist declares, "No God!" The agnostic says, "Maybe God." The adherent asserts, "*My* God!"

In addition to the Type Trio, there is an Attitude Triad to which the caller should also be sensitive in relating to an outsider, whose basic disposition toward what the caller represents may be antagonism, or apathy, or arrogance. The stance of antagonism is, "I don't like!" The stance of apathy is, "I don't care!" The stance of arrogance is, "I don't agree!" which means "You're wrong!"

Any one of the Attitude Triad may go with any one of the Type Trio. The skill in calling is recognizing which type and which attitude one is dealing with and then proceeding in the most appropriate way. Assuming that one has entered into a faith discussion, the conversation with the self-styled atheist might go something like this:

ATHEIST: I don't believe in God.

CALLER: Do you mean you can't believe or you don't want to believe?

ATHEIST: Both!

CALLER: You don't want to believe . . .

ATHEIST: It's unimportant.

CALLER: What if there were a God? Would it be important to you?

ATHEIST: I can't answer that question, because I don't believe in God.

CALLER: You mean you can't believe in God?

ATHEIST: Not the kind of God I hear people talk about.

CALLER: The kind of God you hear people talk about . . .

ATHEIST: Yes, a God who . . . (states his view of God)

CALLER: I couldn't believe in a God like that either. Let me tell you about the God I believe in (states his view of God). Could you believe in a God like that?

ATHEIST: Maybe, but somebody would have to prove him to me first.

CALLER: Nobody can prove the existence of God.

ATHEIST: Then why are you so sure there is a God?

CALLER: Because I wake up believing. It's an assumption of faith. I can't prove it, but I can point to all kinds of evidence that support that assumption. We both start with an assumption, by the way. You assume No God. What evidence is there to support that assumption?

ATHEIST: All the evil in the world, for one thing.

CALLER: That's a real problem for me, too, but faith has its answers that satisfy those who want to believe. The real question for each of us is, Do I want to believe? If I really want to, in time I will. But that doesn't mean that I won't have doubts.

ATHEIST: You mean you have doubts too?

CALLER: I sure do. Everyone does, if one's really honest. Faith without doubt is no longer faith. It would then be knowledge. Faith implies doubt. Faith is always seeking.

ATHEIST: In that case, there may even be hope for me!

CALLER: And for me! And for anyone who is sincerely seeking the truth.

ATHEIST: I think I'm a seeker.

CALLER: Then it's not a case of not wanting to believe.

ATHEIST: I suppose not, when you come right down to it.

CALLER: In that case, sincerity would mean checking out the possibility that there just may be a God. How would you like to come to church with me this Sunday? The minister is beginning a series of sermons on the meaning of faith.

ATHEIST: I'll think about it.

It is impossible, of course, to predict how any given conversation will go, and it would be futile to try to structure a set of responses that would be appropriate for every conceivable question that could arise. The imaginary conversation outlined above is intended simply to illustrate a style and a tone of interpersonal witnessing, in which the caller enters into dialogue with the other person, rather than following a set pattern that has been prepared in advance, reinforced by certain memorized Scripture passages.

If the other person is identified as an agnostic, the caller will again want to ask at some point, "Do you want to believe?" and "What would it take to make you believe in God?" The difference between the agnostic and the atheist is usually a matter of attitude; the agnostic is not inclined to be as militant or as negative as the atheist.

The adherent is a different kind of challenge entirely. This is the person who belligerently espouses some other religion or philosophy of his or her own making and whose mind is completely closed to any other ideas. I am not talking about a God-fearing person of another faith, one who is spiritually sensitive and willing to embrace the truth wherever he finds it. Calling on such a person can be a mutually edifying and inspiring faith-sharing experience. Rather, I am talking about the religious bigot, whose narrow-mindedness and lack of spirituality present a difficult challenge. The main thing for the caller to remember is *not to argue!* The caller should be alert to whatever points of contact emerge in the course of the conversation. A nondirective approach is especially needed in this type of call, and the hope is that in reaching out to such people in love, the dividing wall of hostility can be broken down and communication can take place.

Not all outsiders are antagonistic, apathetic, or arrogant. Many will respond positively and enthusiastically. They sincerely want to believe. They want to be convinced. Theirs is the honest, humble doubt of a seeker, not the arrogant, cynical doubt of a skeptic. If it has been a faith-sharing experience, and if the callers feel comfortable in so doing, they may offer the person an opportunity to make a decision for Christ, or to reaffirm his or her faith. It is always appropriate in that case to offer to conclude with prayer, and it is also important for the person to confirm his or her intentions by some specific outward act. The signing of a commitment card serves that purpose for some.

But that is only the beginning of one's discipleship. The decision our Ambassadors are hoping for is a promise to attend the inquirers class, and the outward act that confirms the intention is showing up for the class! The biggest problem with most outsiders is procrastination. It is not doubt but delay that is deadly. They haven't rejected the thought of joining a church; they just haven't gotten around to it. They don't say "No," they say "Maybe." They don't say they won't, they say "We'll think about it," and they will go on thinking about it forever, unless someone can bring them to the point of decision.

We hope that is what the callers will be able, with God's help, to do. They will try to help the procrastinator to acknowledge that anyone who is sincerely seeking God will want to go where the answers are to be found, at least to explore the possibility. A commitment to Christ should be made with integrity, and integrity demands that a person know what it means to be a disciple of Christ and a member of the body of Christ. For me a commitment to Jesus Christ must include a commitment to the church which Christ loved, and for which he died.

A word of caution should be added here, however, about a trap into which almost all inexperienced callers fall. It is the peril of trying to "sell" the church. There is a big difference between faith-sharing and church-selling. One of the lessons that P.R.O.O.F. seminar participants learn is that it is much easier to make a case for God than for Second Presbyterian Church. Mr. and Mrs. Outsider can think of a reason to counter every selling point you mention:

CALLER says: We have a very active program.

OUTSIDER thinks: (We're busy enough as it is.)

CALLER says: We have a fantastic choir.

OUTSIDER thinks: (I'm not that fond of church music. Besides, I can hear better music on that all-music station.)

CALLER says: You should hear our minister preach. He's terrific!

OUTSIDER thinks: (I like to sleep late on Sunday. If I want to hear a sermon, I can listen to Billy Graham.)

CALLER says: Everybody says Second Presbyterian is a very friendly church.

OUTSIDER thinks: (I like the friends I have.)

CALLER says: We'd love to have you worship with us some Sunday.

OUTSIDER *says:* We might very well do that.

CALLER *thinks:* (They're really interested in our church.)

But the chances are that Mr. and Mrs. Outsider will never darken the door of the church. They smiled and nodded politely as the callers paraded the church's virtues, but if those things really counted with the Outsiders, they wouldn't be outsiders. Unchurched people can think of all kinds of reasons for not "buying" the church. The best way to sell the church is for its members to show that the church cares by caring themselves. The goal of a servant church is not to sell itself, but to give itself away.

Church-selling is a barrier to faith-sharing. As long as the subject is Second Presbyterian, the callers will be doing the talking. Far better that Mr. and Mrs. Outsider have a chance to talk about what *they* think, and how they feel, and where they hurt.

The effectiveness of a call, therefore, is not proved by producing a signed commitment card. One could elicit a decision for Christ from someone without ever discovering a person's need or pain. It is for this reason that in evaluating a call, we don't ask our Ambassadors, "Did you get a commitment for Christ?" Instead, after leaving the home the callers are supposed to ask themselves these questions:

Was the conversation meaningful?
Did they "open up" with us?
Was it a faith-sharing experience?

If the answer to each question is yes, then it was a "successful" call. There are three other questions that must then be asked in regard to "following through":

What need, if any, did we discover?
What can we or the church do to be helpful?
What is the next step?

Regardless of the type or attitude, a caller, when encountering resistance, should try to discover the hidden agenda. Things are seldom what they appear to be at first glance, nor are they the same as they are initially described. The backslider's excuse is usually not the real reason for the backsliding. The person may say, "I don't like the music," or something else, when the real reason may be an extramarital affair and the inability to reconcile churchgoing with a guilty conscience. The caller must be as wise as a serpent and as innocent as a dove! He or she does not take everything at face value, and does not assume that every statement is a lie. The caller simply adopts a tentative stance in evaluating whatever information is received.

That requires tact. The caller can't openly show skepticism, either by words or by body language: "Oh, come on now! What's the real reason?" Rather, it is a matter of unspoken awareness, of sensitivity and discernment in assessing where people are, so that one does not respond to the wrong information, as too many callers do. Backsliders know that in the game of self-justification, as in basketball, the best defense is a good offense. And so they criticize and complain to cover up their own shortcomings. The fact is, there is no legitimate excuse for backsliding. A wise caller does not get trapped into dealing with phony issues.

On the other hand, the caller should be looking for whatever element of truth there is in the other person's argument or complaint. The caller tries to identify points of contact in order to build bridges of understanding. When you grant the other person a reasonable point, it is remarkable how often the person will immediately soften his or her position, or reciprocate by acknowledging the reasonableness of your position too.

Occasionally, but judiciously, you can remonstrate, not by arguing but by reasoning. To do this you have to have a specific to deal with. You can't combat generalities. Here is a sample of how such a conversation may go:

OUTSIDER: I have no use for the institutional church. (general statement)

CALLER: What is it that you don't like about the church? (asks for a specific)

OUTSIDER: I can't stand church people. (still too general)

CALLER: You don't like church people. . . . (nondirective leading)

OUTSIDER: No, they're only interested in themselves. (specific: their lack of concern for others)

CALLER: But we're church people, and we wouldn't have come back again if we weren't interested in you. (points out inconsistency of the criticism)

OUTSIDER: I appreciate that, and I admit there are some decent church folks. (acknowledges the reasonable point)

The caller has appealed to reason and made her point not by counterargument or defensive denial, but by helping the outsider to see the obvious exception to his blanket criticism.

Some people, however, are totally unreasonable. They are never willing to grant the other person a reasonable point. If that is the case, you can't do much. If someone simply refuses to talk or is completely unreasonable and unresponsive, the only thing you can do is what Jesus told his disciples to do: "Shake off the dust!" Don't waste time in religious "bull sessions." If the conversation is obviously getting nowhere, take your leave as graciously as possible.

But, keep that person's card in the cultivation file. The person is someone whom your supportive prayer groups should be including in their intercessory prayers. I believe in the power of prayer. If the evangelistic effort is undergirded constantly by the prayers of all, and particularly the prayers of those who see this as their special contribution to the program, miraculous things will happen. Callers will report time and again the feeling that "we were meant to be where we were tonight!" The unexpected joy of a delayed response, the repeated miracle of changed lives, the awareness of being used by God to meet a need, the sense of divine guidance in the midst of many a difficult visit, the countless providential circumstances encountered week by week as the church reaches out to its community, and neighbors are no longer strangers but friends, are abundant evidence of the power of prayer and the presence of God. So do not give up on any outsider. Once you have encountered an outsider, that person is your concern until he or she moves away, joins a church, or dies.

In time, but not too soon, the outsider should be called upon again. It is amazing what a different response you may receive the second or third or fourth time. Never underestimate the power of the Holy Spirit, who gives the increase to the seeds which your callers have planted and watered. You and I cannot change a person's heart, but God can—and does! And God uses us in the process. Most evangelistic programs are not persistent enough to discover that persistence pays off. The hardest hearts are melted, not by your repetition of clever arguments, but by your being there and caring, "fleshing out" the message—the incarnational approach!

7

Role-Playing

I. THE TRAINING TASK

The incarnational approach requires a different set of skills from those taught in a typical propositional style of evangelism. The skills needed are the ability, not to memorize a presentation, but to relate to a person; not to convince someone else to believe, but to understand one's own faith; not to win arguments, but to help people. The training task, therefore, is not a matter of teaching people the right words to say, but a matter of helping them to discover their own faith and to share it. The challenge is how to teach someone to listen, to care, to love. I'm not sure it can be done, but the P.R.O.O.F. seminar is at least an attempt to show what it *means* to listen and to care, and how a loving person responds to need.

The most effective training technique for this purpose is unquestionably *role-playing.* Because of its importance as a training method I am devoting a separate chapter to a discussion of role-playing, with specific application to its use in a P.R.O.O.F. seminar. Before turning to that topic, however, I need to point out that there are preliminary exercises that can be used to help people discover and practice the kinds of skills mentioned above.

II. The Facts Game

One small-group exercise, for example, is a variation of
the familiar Facts Game, in which the participants are
asked to share with the other members of their small
groups four unusual facts about themselves, three of which
are entirely true and one entirely false. The object of the
game is for each person to try to fool the others, while
their purpose is to see if they can guess which is the false
fact for each of the others in the group. The leader in-
structs the groups to avoid giving the false fact away by the
order or the way in which they tell their facts, and not to
"cheat" by making the false fact true in all but one minor
detail.

When all the members of a group have written down
their four facts, each person takes a turn reading his or her
facts to the other members, who are not permitted to ask
for any additional information. Then each member
guesses which fact is the false one. When all have guessed,
but not before, the person who has shared the facts then
tells the correct answer. It is important to let each member of the group guess before giving away the answer.
Then the process is repeated, with the next person reading his or her facts, everybody guessing and then being
told the correct answer, and so on around the entire
group.

This is a wonderful game for loosening up people and
helping them to get acquainted. At first the groups are
fairly quiet, as they try to think of the facts they want to
use, but the noise level gets louder and louder, with
shrieks of laughter sounding throughout the room as the
members of the groups discover hilarious things about the
others in their group and share the fun and embarrassment of guessing wrong most of the time.

In the meantime the leader is wandering around the

room, observing the process and inconspicuously eaves-
dropping on some of the groups. When all the groups are
finished, the leader invites each group to share with the
others some of the unusual things they learned about the
members of their own group.

I always ask if anyone was able to guess right every time,
and that has happened only once or twice in the scores of
times I have used this exercise. I also ask if anyone was able
to fool everyone, and many usually do, whereupon I compliment them for being such good liars.

Then I ask what they learned from the experience. Collectively they will normally come up with certain standard
observations: that people are interesting, that everyone is
unique, that their initial impressions of people are often
wrong, that they can be fooled by outward appearances,
and that their own lives are interesting, too. At this point
I ask them what they learned about their ability to listen.
That question usually comes as a surprise to them, until I
ask them to reflect on their own feelings as they were
listening to each other. Were they eager to hear more?
Was their curiosity aroused to the point where it was hard
for them to go on to the next person? Did they find themselves wanting to know many more details concerning the
facts they were given? Or were they more interested in
getting to their turn and sharing their own facts?

I ask them what happened when everyone in the group
had finished. Did they sit around twiddling their thumbs
and wondering what to do next? Some do, and that certainly says something about their interest in other people.
The better listeners they are, the longer it takes to play the
game, and the best clue to their listening ability is what
happens when they finish! The lesson to be learned, therefore, is that people are indeed interesting, and a good
listener will discover that faster than others, because most
people are eager to talk about themselves to anyone who
will listen.

III. An Exercise in Faith-Sharing

The Facts Game is an excellent warm-up for the next small-group exercise, which is an experience in faith-sharing. Having already dealt with the cognitive material relating to the meaning of faith and the paradox of the gift and the grasp, they are now ready to talk about *why* they believe in God. Each person is given three minutes to share his or her faith with the others in the group. The atmosphere is entirely different from the frivolity of the Facts Game. All are intensely serious and sincere, as they quietly relate to the members in their small group the evidence of God's presence in their lives.

I ask them to be fair with their time, and I use a pitch pipe to signal the end of each three-minute period. When all have shared, I allow them to continue talking for another ten or fifteen minutes, and they are always reluctant to stop when I finally call a halt to the exercise. The general discussion that follows is always instructive and revealing. "What did you learn from this experience?" I ask, and the answers are always the same: that people are beautiful as well as interesting, that they really feel close to one another after sharing their faith, that everyone's experience is different, and yet they all have the same kinds of reasons for believing in God.

"Were you talking about *why* you believe or *what* you believe?" I ask them, and they quickly assure me they were talking about the why of their faith. "Can you see the difference now?" Without hesitation they reply, "Definitely!"

"Was anybody preaching?" The answer is almost always No, although every now and then a few get carried away and start talking about what they believe instead of why. That's when it begins to sound like preaching, which is all right in the pulpit, but not in the living room. "Was it

difficult for you to talk about why you believe in God?"
Again the answer is usually No, but some will admit that
they thought it would be. "Was it a meaningful experience?" The answer to that one is invariably Yes! So much
so, in fact, that some are moved to tears as they share with
one another the things God has done in their lives.

They have now discovered that they can share their
faith and that they have a faith to share. For some it is like
the dawn of a new day to discover that they can speak with
authority about their own experience, and they don't have
to be theologians or Greek scholars to have something
valid and helpful to say. Earlier in the seminar they had
wrestled with the meaning of faith; now they have experienced it. They have been introduced to a new concept
of evangelism with which they are beginning to feel comfortable, and now they are ready to try it out in some
role-playing.

IV. DISCOVERING ROLE-PLAYING

I am really enthusiastic about the value of role-playing
as a training tool for service evangelism. My discovery of
its effectiveness as an educational tool was almost acciden-
tal. While conducting a workshop on interpersonal witnessing for a group of United Presbyterian ministers in
Arlington, Texas, I declared myself to be an agnostic and
invited one of the participants to assume the role of a
church caller. There followed an intense encounter in our
imaginary living room as the two of us became completely
oblivious to the other thirty persons who were observing
the dialogue.

When the "call" was completed and we returned to
reality, I was at first chagrined and embarrassed to discover we had consumed more than an hour! But in the
discussion that followed I was completely amazed at the
response of the group. They had identified vicariously
with the two of us and were totally involved in the experi-

ence, though not one of them had said a word for an hour!
I asked them to be completely frank: Was it helpful? "Ab-
solutely!" was the unanimous response.

Their reaction was a confirmation, not of the length of
time, but of the method, which was immensely effective
in spite of the lengthiness of the experience. From then on
I began doing more and more with role-playing, and I
have found it to be a most effective method of leadership
training in various communication and interpersonal relations skills.

My knowledge of this tool until this writing had been
entirely experiential. I had read nothing about the theory
or practice of role-playing, nor had I ever attempted to
express my own ideas on the subject in any cognitive way.
My research has reconfirmed my own conviction of the
usefulness of role-playing.

Properly used, role-playing is a powerful tool. It requires
flexibility and spontaneity on the part of the players. They
should be told that they do not have to stick rigidly to the
situation as it was described in the beginning, but that
they are free to interact with one another as behavioral
changes are experienced or other subtle stimuli are introduced.

Before breaking up into small groups, there may be a
trial run by a volunteer or a selected demonstration group,
which can serve as a practice model for the other groups.
The role-playing activity takes place near the end of the
seminar, when interpersonal relationships have had time
to develop and there has been a balance of content and
discussion, leader input and group participation, intellectual and relational activity.

V. The Role of the Leader

The role of the leader is crucial to the success of any
role-playing activity. It is the leader's responsibility to prepare the group for the role-playing experience, to decide

which type of activity is most appropriate to his or her purpose, to set the stage for the participants with adequate but not excessive instructions, to control the timing and termination of the enactments, and to conduct the evaluation process at the end.

I have come to believe that the ability to be a good group leader is as much a gift of God as it is an acquired skill. Some people have had plenty of training and know all the rules but don't seem to be as effective as others who have had no training whatsoever. The latter are able to accomplish by intuition, native intelligence, and a sensitivity to people, what others struggle without success to learn to do.

At the same time, I realize that given the necessary intelligence and sensitivity, anyone should be able to profit from the experience and expertise of others, whatever the skill he or she may be seeking to acquire. For this reason some training in group dynamics, interpersonal communication, and other skills related to small-group leadership would be helpful to someone leading any role-playing activity, and especially in the evaluation process. Some specific suggestions for leaders and observers are included in the following section, which is a description of the use of role-playing in the P.R.O.O.F. model of evangelism training.

VI. ROLE-PLAYING AND P.R.O.O.F.

Before discussing the use of role-playing in a P.R.O.O.F. seminar, I feel that it is necessary to describe briefly how it fits into the format of the seminar (see Chapter 8).

P.R.O.O.F. is designed as a fifteen-hour experience, with an optimum number of thirty participants. The first hour is spent in getting acquainted, using some relational experiences to facilitate the process. There is then some cognitive input on the meaning of faith, followed by group discussion, in which the participants examine their own definitions in the context of the paradox of faith as "gift" and "grasp" (see Chapter 2, II. C). There follows some further input on the various modern challenges to faith.

After a coffee break, and without any advance notice or warning, I assume the role of an unbeliever who wanders into the group and challenges the participants to tell me why they believe in God. This is their first taste of role-playing and, without exception, they become involved in the situation in a matter of seconds. After thirty minutes or so we then discuss the experience. The group is invariably unanimous in acknowledging complete ineffectiveness in dealing with the "stranger." The first evening ends on a discouraging note for some, who have discovered the impossibility of establishing a rational basis for faith that is either normative or logically compelling.

The next night I attempt to help them to recognize, conceptualize, articulate, and confess their faith assumptions. They are then ready to examine, with integrity, the evidence that tends to support those assumptions, and from there to consider the implications of all of this for sharing faith. That leads to a discussion of the meaning and validity of evangelism and an attempt to clarify some of the misconceptions and confusion in the use of the term.

Now we are ready to face the question of methodology and to present a particular style and approach called service evangelism, which is incarnational rather than propositional, person-centered rather than convert-centered, need-related rather than a memorized "spiel." In relating the outreach to the needs of the community and to the "whole person," we attempt to bridge the gap between social action and personal salvation, and to dispel what I believe is an unfortunate and unnecessary dichotomy.

By now we are well into the third and final session, which is an all-day meeting, and the group is ready for some practical training in the art of evangelistic calling, in the style previously described. For this purpose I make extensive use of role-playing, using at least four hours in the process, with careful critique and analysis following each simulated situation. The seminar ends with a brief wrap-up and a sharing of feelings about the overall experience.

Having looked hurriedly at the format of the seminar, we can now turn to role-playing, starting with some thoughts on the structure.

A. Structuring

At the time of registration, each participant receives a name tag with a letter and a number in the upper left corner, and with a (usually) different-colored dot in each of the other corners. The letter (A, B, C, D, or E) identifies the person as a member of a group of five for role-playing purposes. The number (between 1 and 30, where thirty are present) identifies the person individually. The three colors will be used to assign the person to a different group at each of the three sessions. (See Small-Group Rotation Chart, p. 131.) Before dividing the participants into small groups for the role-playing activity, the leader gives brief instructions and explains the process. At this time the leader tells the group that role-playing, to be effective, requires the following:

Involvement. Ignore the observers. Don't play to the audience. Relax and let go. Don't be self-conscious and inhibited. Keep in character—don't drop in and out of the scene.

Empathy. Enter into the role. Don't project your own attitudes, prejudices, and hang-ups onto the other person. Be the person you are playing, not yourself (unless that is your role). Try sincerely to believe and to feel as that person does.

Consistency. Assume a characterization and stick to it. Your responses should be consistent with the character of the person you are portraying. Be realistic and believable in the role. Don't invent a new fact to counter every reasonable argument of the other person. Be consistent.

Flexibility. Be flexible! Be ready to note and respond to subtle changes that occur in the situation—hints of need, points of contact, opportunities for witness, etc. Let the situation flow and develop naturally.

The leader then explains that the people will be divided into groups of five ("All those with a blue dot in the upper right corner of their name tag go to the group of chairs by the blue dot on the wall"). The groups may be located in different parts of a large room, or in different rooms. For each situation to be enacted, there will be two callers, two "residents," and an "observer." Roles are switched by number or letter in each new situation, all of these logistics having been worked out in advance by the leader to assure that everyone has an equal opportunity to play each role.

The leader calls the two residents (persons to be called upon) into a huddle and gives each team a card containing a brief written description of a situation. For example: "You are an elderly couple, unchurched, alone in the world, unable to care for yourselves adequately, desperately in need of help but don't know where or how to turn for it." The rest is left to the imagination of the players. The callers are told only that they are calling for the church on homes in the neighborhood; they have only a name from the Reverse Street Telephone Directory. The observer can be told either what the residents are told or nothing more than the callers. There are advantages either way, and I have used both.

The four role-players are to ignore the observer, who is not to speak, react, or interact with them in any way, but is to be as inconspicuous as possible. The observer may take notes, however. The callers are asked to complete their calls in fifteen minutes, making their exit in whatever manner seems appropriate. They may, for example, want to offer a prayer. Some of the experiences are extremely moving. If necessary, the leader calls a halt and asks the observers to share their observations with their groups, pointing out the good things and raising questions (in a nonthreatening way) about how the situation might have been handled differently. The participants can then respond to the observer's comments, do some self-evaluation, and discuss the experience among themselves.

The leader should allow at least five minutes for this process, but not let it go on too long. It is better to repeat the process more often with different situations. After the small-group discussions the leader can then ask for general comments or questions. The leader may want to make a few *brief* suggestions at this time, underlining any general lessons to be drawn from the experience. It is always interesting and helpful to find out if the callers were able to discover the need behind the door, and if not, why not.

After this very brief evaluation process, the leader tells the group members to switch roles according to the numbering system used and calls the new sets of residents into a huddle. (See Role-Playing Rotation Chart.) The leader then distributes to the new residents a second set of cards describing the situation they are to enact, and the process is repeated all over again. All the enactments can be taken from real-life situations.

ROLE-PLAYING ROTATION CHART

ROLE-PLAYING SITUATION		1	2	3	4	5	6	7	8	9	10
OBSERVER	A		B	C	D	E	A	B	C	D	E
CALLERS	BC		CD	DE	EA	AB	BD	CE	DA	EB	AC
RESIDENTS	DE		EA	AB	BC	CD	CE	DA	EB	AC	BD

[Letters in boldface indicate the lead person]

It should be remembered that prior to the role-playing activity there has been considerable instruction by the leader on the technique of calling. One of the callers has been assigned the lead role and the other the supportive role on each call. They have been asked to have a brief prayer before they ring the doorbell, and they have been told what to say when the door is opened, where to sit in the living room, what to do if the television is on, how to deal with someone who is totally unreasonable, how to handle questions they can't answer, and so forth. All these instructions have much more meaning for the participants after they have done some role-playing.

Role-playing in the P.R.O.O.F. seminar is a kind of "sensitivity training"—teaching people to care. The question to which I am still seeking an answer is whether an insensitive person can be taught to be sensitive, or a callous person can be taught to care. My partial answer is that we can at least help one another to see what a sensitive person does in a given situation, and how a caring person behaves. Probably we have to rely on God to do the rest, for my faith tells me that only God can change human hearts. But maybe role-playing is a way of helping God to do his thing. It is worth trying, at any rate.

B. Suggestions for Leaders

Although I recognize these human limitations, I should like, nevertheless, to offer the following practical suggestions for leaders, to facilitate a more effective use of role-playing in general:

1. Always address the participants by their role names when discussing a particular scene or situation. This rule applies before, during, and after the enactment. ("How did you feel when Mr. Jones slammed the door in your face?")

2. Don't let a player drop out of character and address you or the observer. Always direct the player back to the scene. ("Tell that to the caller, Mr. Jones.")

3. Help the players to get over their self-consciousness

by doing bits of role-playing yourself, as I did in the scene with the agnostic stranger who invaded the P.R.O.O.F. seminar. In a demonstration enactment (i.e., one in which the rest of the group is observing a few players), it is wise to ask for volunteers for the parts.

4. Don't allow a scene to drag on if it is getting nowhere. Stop and begin again with a new scene, or with different players, or with some other variation.

5. In conducting the follow-up discussion, help the players to see the meaning or significance of what is happening by asking appropriate questions. "Did you discover anything about your ability to persuade someone to join the church? Were you able to discover a need in which you or the church could help? Did you learn anything about your ability to listen? Were you believable? Were the others believable?"

6. In the general discussion these findings may be mentioned by members of the different groups, or the leader may have to draw them out by more questions, or restate them to focus on the important lessons to be learned.

7. Ask for feedback on the process each time and deal with any problems or questions that may occur.

8. Don't be judgmental. This is not the time for evaluating the role-playing performances, except when compliments are in order. Praise encourages the players and enhances their involvement.

9. Help the group to make the application to their own life situations. In the P.R.O.O.F. seminars it is extremely easy for the players to do this, as the situations are so realistic, and two of the players are always playing themselves.

For role-playing in general the main purposes of the postmortem discussion are to give the players an opportunity to verbalize insights gained from the experience, to let them express feelings generated by the experience, to help them generalize from their insights to other aspects of their lives, and to give the onlookers a chance to express their feelings caused by their identification with the players.

There are as many different ways to use role-playing as there are ideas in a fertile imagination. In the final analysis, the value of role-playing can be discovered only by doing it. The best advertisement for role-playing, as for almost anything else, is satisfied customers—of whom I am one.

8

Conducting a P.R.O.O.F. Seminar

You will gain great satisfaction from conducting your first evangelism training seminar. This book is intended to serve as a "textbook" for those who would like to use the P.R.O.O.F. model as well as for those who attend. Provided you understand and agree with the conceptual rationale for faith-sharing and service evangelism and with the style of interpersonal witnessing described in the previous chapters, and assuming, of course, that you have some people ready, willing, and able to attend a seminar, you should be able to "carry it off," with this chapter serving as your guide. The P.R.O.O.F. approach lends itself to easy adaptation, so that each leader can modify the format or the time schedule to suit his or her own situation. In other words, use the principles, but present them in your way.

I. PRELIMINARIES

A. Recruiting the Participants
In my early P.R.O.O.F. seminars all the prospective participants were personally invited by me to attend. Those who responded received a follow-up letter confirming the dates and times, enclosing an outline of the format, and suggesting some questions to which they were to give

some thought in advance of the first session (Appendix B).

After the first two seminars, I had developed a list of persons who had been unable to accept the invitation to participate, but who had indicated interest in being asked again. For the next seminar these would receive a form letter, with a self-addressed return postcard. If they responded positively, they then received a personalized follow-up letter with the usual information and inserts.

The recruitment function has since been taken over by a volunteer, who makes telephone calls to a list of names which she gets from me. I then receive a written report of the results of her calls, and more names are supplied if needed. She herself is an enthusiastic P.R.O.O.F. "graduate" and does an excellent job of interpreting the nature and purpose of the seminar. Those who agree to attend receive the usual personalized letter from me.

I believe in setting the registration fee as low as possible for our own church members, but high enough to include food costs, materials, and a copy of this book, *Service Evangelism*, for each couple and single person. The books are distributed at the end of the seminar.

When the reservations are complete, a list of the names is sent to each registrant. It is important that the total be divisible by five, because of the small-group activities, including the role-playing that takes place on Saturday (see Chapter 7, VI. A). I always try to have alternates available in case of any last-minute cancellations, and I impress upon all the registrants the necessity of their being present for every session.

B. Scheduling the Seminar

In deciding how best to schedule the required fifteen hours I considered several alternatives: a series of five three-hour evening meetings; a weekend program, calling for nine hours on Saturday and six hours on Sunday; a Friday evening, all day Saturday, and Saturday evening program; two successive Saturdays totaling fifteen hours.

The plan I eventually chose called for us to meet for three
and a half hours on Thursday night and Friday night, and
eight hours on Saturday. This plan seems to work out best
for most people, and fits well with the format. The interval
between Thursday night and Friday night is a convenient
and helpful period for the participants to reflect upon the
first session, which is a provocative if not threatening experience for most of them, while the back-to-back Friday
night and Saturday sessions help to establish a retreat atmosphere.

C. Setting Up the Room

All the sessions are held in the same room, which is large
enough for the entire group to meet in a central circle,
with space for six small groups around the periphery of the
room, far enough apart to avoid intergroup distractions.

On Thursday afternoon I supervise the arrangement of
the chairs, which should be of a fairly comfortable style,
inasmuch as the participants will be sitting for most of the
time. We use couches and cushioned chairs for the large-
group circle, and folding chairs for the small groups. The
lighting should be subdued but ample, with a table lamp
or standing lamp by each small group and enough light on
the center circle for the people to be able to take notes.
I like to have two portable blackboards, plenty of newsprint, and several felt-tipped pens of colors to match the
colors assigned to the various groups. Each small group is
identified by a large colored dot on the wall. Use masking
tape to avoid marring the walls.

D. Preparing for Small-Group Activities

Much care and thought is given to the small-group assignments. I try to divide the sexes as evenly as possible,
to mix the ages and personality types, and to give the
participants opportunities to be with as many different
persons as possible during the course of the seminar. (See
Small-Group Rotation Chart.) The name tags are prepared

accordingly, with a letter and a number in one corner, and a colored dot in each of the other three corners. (See Chapter 7, VI. A.) During the seminar the people are asked at different times to go to the group of chairs by the dot that matches the dot in one of the corners of their name tag. The letters are used in the role-playing activity, as described in Chapter 7, VI. A. The people are asked to turn in their name tags each evening, to be sure that they are available for use throughout the seminar. Otherwise some are sure to be left at home.

SMALL-GROUP ROTATION CHART

		Orange	Red	Black	Purple	Blue	Green
	A	1	2	3	4	5	6
	B	7	8	9	10	11	12
SESSION 1	C	13	14	15	16	17	18
	D	19	20	21	22	23	24
	E	25	26	27	28	29	30
	A	1	6	11	16	21	26
	B	2	7	12	17	22	27
SESSION 2	C	3	8	13	18	23	28
	D	4	9	14	19	24	29
	E	5	10	15	20	25	30
	A	6	12	1	2	13	25
	B	5	7	14	22	23	3
SESSION 3	C	16	20	27	9	8	28
	D	15	21	18	29	4	11
	E	26	17	10	19	30	24

[Numbers in boldface indicate women]

The leader supplies each small group with a felt-tipped pen in a color to match their identifying dot, to be used in writing their shared expectations, composite definitions, and other assignments. The newsprint sheets are

then affixed to the wall behind their chairs, and by the end
of the seminar there is a rather colorful display of their
mental productivity. I save these sheets and identify them
by their P.R.O.O.F. number (P-I, P-II, P-III, etc.) These are
prominently displayed around the room so that, as the various assignments are completed, the participants can see
how their own ideas compare with those of their prede-
cessors.

Some appropriate way to signal the end of each group
activity is needed. I use a pitch pipe and the wall clock, but
a timer is also a good device for this purpose. I also use a
piano for one or two "musical exercise" breaks, when the
group marches around in a circle, each person beating in
rhythm, to the tune I play on the piano, on the back of the
person in front of him. This is a "fun" way to loosen people
up and to wake them up (!) on Saturday morning, for
example. There is always spontaneous applause at the end
of the exercise. If you do not play the piano, perhaps you
can ask someone else to do so, and if there is no piano, the
participants can sing as they walk.

E. Providing for Food and Other Essentials

Cookies and beverages are provided for the evening
meetings, and a continental breakfast and a good lunch
are served on Saturday. You will need someone to prepare
the meals, preferably a good cook! The Saturday lunch
hour has always been a meaningful part of the seminar.

The participants have been asked to bring a Bible with
them, and materials for taking notes, but I always have a
few extra Bibles and paper and pencils on hand for those
who may have forgotten. There should be a few low tables
within the large circle, including one in front of the
leader's chair, for whatever materials you plan to distribute, and for your own reference books and notes. Other
useful items will be added as the need arises.

F. Greeting the Arrivers

The seminar leader should be the first to arrive each night and on Saturday morning, to see that everything is in order and to greet the participants as they arrive. On the first night you will want to introduce the participants to one another, since you will usually be the only person who knows everyone. Encourage them to mingle and get acquainted. When all have arrived and had their cup of coffee or tea, invite them to take a seat in the large circle —and the P.R.O.O.F. seminar is ready to begin.

II. OUTLINE FOR THE SEMINAR LEADER

The following is my outline for a typical P.R.O.O.F. seminar with the suggested times for each segment. I must emphasize that the leader should be flexible and able to adjust to particular needs or problems that arise. You may have to take more time on some parts and less on others. The content of the teaching portions of the seminar has been covered in the earlier chapters of this book.

OUTLINE FOR THE SEMINAR LEADER

THURSDAY NIGHT

7:00 P.M.

I. Introduction

  A. Getting Acquainted—Who are we?

    1. Greet arrivers. Give out name tags. Have coffee and tea ready. Participants mingle and chat informally.

    2. Gather the group together to sit in the central circle. Offer a short prayer.

    3. Who am I? Have the members of the group tell

the basic facts about themselves. You begin—in order to set the pace.

4. After everyone has shared, ask, "Who knows something nice about___?" (People become very affirmative of one another.) Make sure everyone is mentioned.

8:15 P.M.
Coffee Break. Ask the participants to get acquainted with someone they hadn't known before.

8:30 P.M.
B. Sharing Expectations—Where are we?
1. Divide into small groups, saying, "Go to the dot that matches the color in the upper right corner of your name tag."
2. Have each person write his or her answer to this question: What would I like to happen to me in the seminar?
3. Have each person share his or her expectations with the other members of the small group.
4. Have each small group make a composite list of expectations.
5. Make a complete composite list for the entire seminar. You write them down on newsprint.

8:55 P.M.
C. Stating the Purpose—Why are we?
1. Quickly review the composite list you have put up on the wall, and indicate your own expectations regarding each of *their* expectations.
2. State the purpose of the seminar: To explore the meaning of faith, to experience the reality of faith, to establish a method of sharing faith.
3. "This is only a beginning." Let them know that the seminar will be partly informational, partly motivational, partly reflectional.

9:00 P.M.

II. The Meaning of Faith

A. Defining Faith—What is faith?

1. Same small groups as before. Have each person write his or her answer to, What is faith?

2. Have each person share his or her definition with the others in the small group.

3. Have each group develop a composite definition and write it on the top half of the newsprint sheet, using their color.

9:25 P.M. Break, stretch, and return to circle.

9:30 P.M.

B. Having Faith—When is faith?

1. Enter the "stranger"! Role-play an agnostic and press the group members to tell you why they believe in God. Be polite and pleasant, but reject all their tautologies. Respond with interest to those who share their experiences. Give hints of personal need, but not too soon or too obviously, to see if the group will show concern, etc.

10:00 P.M.

2. Break role-play. Review the process. The participants know they couldn't persuade the stranger and they usually feel frustrated and discouraged. Ask some leading questions to help them to see that they didn't try to discover the stranger's needs, or show concern for the stranger as a person. Help the group members to see that they were talking about *what* they believed, not *why,* and that their "reasons" were not proof to the stranger.

3. "Any final comments or reactions?"

10:25 P.M. Stand, join hands around the circle, and invite the participants to say aloud whatever single words express what is on their hearts at this time.

FRIDAY NIGHT

7:00 P.M. Fellowship Time

7:10 P.M. Review (everyone seated in large circle):
1. Everyone's reflections on the first night.
2. Your reflections on the first night. Compliment
them on their good points: "You were articulate."
"You expressed yourself well." "Some came close to
identifying with the stranger."
3. "There are many others like him out there. If we
are going to reach them, we have to understand our
own faith and establish a valid basis for our beliefs.
Only then will our statements have integrity and
our arguments consistency."
4. Tell them you were "undressing" them theologically. "We must first stand naked before God if we
are to learn the meaning of grace."

7:25 P.M.
B. Having Faith (continued)
4. The Grasp
a. Discuss briefly the struggle of faith, our effort
to reach God.
b. Divide into small groups (different color this
time). Give each group a sheet of paper with
four or five texts that emphasize the "grasp"
(Chapter 2, II. C).
c. Ask the groups to discuss each text briefly.
"Do you see the 'grasp' in each one? Can you
illustrate any of the texts from your own experience? Can you think of other grasp texts?"
d. Mention the leap of faith, but don't develop
the idea yet.
5. The Gift
a. Still in small groups, discuss briefly the gift of
faith. Our effort is always in response to God's
offer. Note whether or not the composite defi-

nitions reflect an emphasis on the grasp aspect of faith. The paradox of faith.

b. Give each group a sheet of paper with four or five texts that emphasize the "gift" (Chapter 2, II. C).

c. Have them discuss the texts briefly. Then point out the difficulty of the concept. "We're dealing with a profound truth, easily stated, hard to comprehend."

d. Have them rewrite or modify their definitions to reflect their new understanding of faith. Use the lower half of the sheet and put it back up on the wall.

8:10 P.M. Coffee Break. Then back to large circle.

8:20 P.M.

6. The Grasp, the Gift, and the Leap

a. Put the Leap of Faith diagram on the board and explain it (Chapter 2, II. D).

b. The leap is our grasp, but the urge to leap is God's gift!

8:40 P.M.

C. Sharing Faith—How is faith?

1. If faith is a gift of God, then how can we "share" it? Cover the principles in Chapter 2, III (Bridging the Gap; Answering the Why?; Justifying the Approach). "We have been probing responsibly!"

9:10 P.M. Break, stretch, return to same small groups.

9:20 P.M.

III. The Reality of Faith—P.R.O.O.F. tests

A. Faith Established—That I Believe

1. The Facts Game. (See Chapter 7, II.) Explain the rules. Give the members five minutes to think of their four facts, two minutes to each member to share the facts.

9:40 P.M.

> 2. Group discussion of the process. "Any unusual facts in the different groups? What did you learn about each other?" etc.

9:50 P.M.

> 3. Stating faith: each participant takes one minute to answer the question, Do I really believe in a personal God? Not why, or what, just whether. Tell the participants to express their doubts, if any.

10:00 P.M.

> 4. *Brief* comments on the above experience. Does everyone believe in a personal God? Does anyone have doubts? (Note the reality and universality of doubt.)

10:05 P.M.

> B. Faith Experienced—Why I believe
> 1. Same small groups. Each person says, "I, _____ _____, believe in God because . . ." and takes three minutes to complete the statement. Tell the group to be fair in the use of time!

10:20 P.M.

> 2. Reflect on the experience. Ask: "What were your impressions of the others in your group? Were you talking about *what* you believe or *why* you believe? Was anybody 'preaching'? Were the others in your group convincing? appealing? sincere? Were you tuned in, or turned off? Do you see the validity of 'sharing the confirming evidence of your faith assumption'? Have you 'experienced faith' tonight?"

10:29 P.M. Ask the members of the seminar to join hands in their small groups and close with sentence prayers.

SATURDAY

8:30 A.M. Continental breakfast. Ask each person upon arriving to fill out "bench mark" sheet. (Appendix C.)

8:45 A.M. Take places in large circle and sing the Doxology. Ask each person what he or she has to praise God for this morning. After all have spoken, offer a short prayer of thanksgiving and then sing the Doxology again.

8:55 A.M. Review (everyone seated).
We have gotten acquainted, shared our expectations, stated, and by now should understand, the purpose of the seminar: "Probing Responsibly Our Own Faith." We have discussed the meaning of faith—in depth! We have experienced the reality of faith.

9:00 A.M.
C. Faith Understood—What I believe
1. Divide the large group into new small groups (again a different color dot).
Tell the participants they are being interviewed on the radio. Each one has two minutes to summarize the content of his or her faith. Be fair with the use of time!

9:15 A.M.
2. Return to large circle. Ask the participants if they could feel the difference between the *why* and the *what* of their faith.
3. Explain that there has been and will continue to be some "content" throughout the seminar, but that this is not a course in Introductory Theology. That will be another seminar. Nevertheless, they should have a much better understanding of *what* they believe, after the P.R.O.O.F. seminar.

9:20 A.M.

IV. The Sharing of Faith

  A. The Meaning—Defining It

    1. Introductory remarks: The need to share our faith with the world "out there." We are talking about evangelism. How to reach the unchurched, the "outsider," the secular person who is totally indifferent, or apathetic, who couldn't care less about God, Jesus, the church, or anything else pertaining to religion.

    2. Two philosophies the secular person does not know about but is affected by: logical positivism (state the verification principle) and linguistic analysis (discuss the problem of God language). See Chapter 2, III. C.

    3. Can we communicate our faith meaningfully? My experience tells me we can, though we may see some things differently.

    4. The Great Commission—our responsibility to evangelize. Every Christian is called to be a witness (Acts 1:8).

9:30 A.M. Musical Break.

Use piano, musical tape, or record. Form a large circle, turn to the right, and march around the circle as you beat in rhythm on the back of the person in front of you. Change the rhythm as the music changes. Reverse your direction! Now take a five-minute break and then return to your same small groups.

9:40 A.M.

    5. What, then, is evangelism? Tell each group to develop a definition of evangelism. They have ten minutes. Use newsprint and proper color.

9:50 A.M.

    6. Ask groups to read the definitions. Comment briefly, and compliment the group members. Put

the sheets of newsprint up on the wall, and everyone *return to the full circle.*

9:55 A.M.

7. Define and explain the meaning of "service evangelism", and point out briefly the distinctions as
given in Chapter 4.

10:05 A.M.

8. Discuss briefly the example of Paul (Chapter 5).
9. Questions and answers.

10:20 A.M. Break (ten minutes)

10:30 A.M.

B. The Method—Describing it
1. Interpersonal witnessing is basic to all evangelism (see Chapter 6).
2. Some do's and don'ts of interpersonal witnessing.
3. The importance of listening. Discuss briefly the C
Rules of Listening (Chapter 6, VI).
4. Questions and answers.

11:00 A.M. Break (five minutes), then return to same small
group.

11:05 A.M.

C. The Manner—Doing it
1. Give a few brief instructions about role-playing,
then announce that D and E will be the "residents,"
B and C the "callers," and A the "observer." Call all
the D's and E's into the center and give them a card
describing their role: "Backsliders named Jones
haven't been in church for a couple of years. They
give all kinds of excuses, but the real reason is they
are having financial problems, never paid up their
pledge from three years ago, and have a guilty conscience about it. Give a few hints, but don't make
it too obvious." The callers are told only the name,
and that the residents haven't been coming to

church. Find out what's what. The observers are to
be as inconspicuous as possible, take notes, and be
prepared to comment on the calls. B is to take the
lead and C has the supportive role. They are to have
a brief prayer before knocking on the imaginary
door.

2. Allow fifteen minutes for the call, then signal the
callers to make their exits.

3. Observers comment on how the callers did. The
family also comment on how they felt about the
callers' approach. Discuss briefly among yourselves.

4. Get the attention of all the groups and ask them
how it went:

    a. "Did you discover the real reason (i.e., finan-
cial embarrassment)? Were you able to 'win
them back to church'? How did you callers feel
—afraid? self-conscious? insecure? inspired? or
what?"

    b. In evaluating your calls, ask yourselves these
three questions: "Was the conversation meaningful? Did the people open up with us? Was it
a faith-sharing experience?" If the answer to
each of these questions is yes, then it was a
successful call.

    c. In regard to follow-through, there are three
other questions that must be asked: "What
need, if any, did we discover? What can we or
the church do to be helpful? What is the next
step?"

11:35 A.M.

5. Switch roles and call the new residents, C and D,
to the center and give them their role-description
cards. Make up your own situations! For example:
"Unchurched, new in the community, had been
shopping around for a church. They signed a pew
card two Sundays ago, with last name and address

only." The callers have only the pew card information. Follow same procedure. Allow fifteen minutes, then ask observers to comment, and ask the groups to discuss among themselves how it went and what was learned. Use the evaluation questions.

6. Any questions? Make whatever comments are called for.

12:00 NOON. Break for lunch. Fifteen minutes to wash up. We eat in another room around tables arranged in a large rectangle. Ask someone to say grace.

1:00 P.M.

7. Now that they have tried it, here are a few things for them to keep in mind about role-playing. In order to be effective, the players must be:

a. *Involved:* ignore the observer; don't be inhibited.

b. *Empathetic:* enter into the role; be the person you are playing.

c. *Consistent:* assume a characterization and stick to it.

d. *Flexible:* be ready to respond to changes in the situation.

8. Any questions on the process?

1:10 P.M.

9. Using the chart, call the next pair of residents forward, and give them their role-description card —for example: "Unchurched elderly couple, alone, deaf, infirm, and destitute," and repeat the process. Make any necessary teaching comments at the end.

1:30 P.M.

Repeat the process with the fourth situation—for example: "Racially mixed couple. Unchurched. Not sure they would be welcome. Black husband has A.M.E. background; white wife is former Roman Catholic."

1:55 P.M.

Choose another real-life situation.

2:20 P.M.

Sixth situation: Do not admit the callers.

2:30 P.M.

Musical Break. Same as before.

2:35 P.M.

Seventh situation.

3:00 P.M.

Eighth situation.

3:20 P.M.

Ninth situation.

3:40 P.M.

V. Wrap-up

A. Commitment

1. Tell them to move to *second* small group (the Friday-night group).

2. Each one shares "Where I am at this point in my faith." No more than two minutes each!

3. "Go around the circle again and tell the others what you intend to do about it from here on." One minute each.

4:10 P.M.

B. Continuity

1. Return quickly to full circle

2. This is only the beginning. Remember these three P's:

a. "Probe: keep probing your own faith."

b. "Practice: try sharing it with others."

c. "Program: join the Ambassadors! Ask if they will commit at least one night a month to calling for the church."

4:15 P.M.

  C. Conclusion

    1. Closing comments. Review the expectations and see how we made out. Thank the participants for their openness, honesty, etc.

    2. Invite them to share their impressions of the experience.

4:30 P.M.

    3. Join hands around the circle for closing sentence prayers.

    4. Ask them to fill out the evaluation sheet before they leave! (Appendix D)

    5. Distribute copies of this book, *Service Evangelism.*

III. THE EVALUATION PROCESS

P.R.O.O.F. seminars have a built-in evaluation process, including the bench marks, which are filled out by the participants at the halfway point, and the evaluation sheets, which are filled out at the end of the seminar. The comments of the participants have been extremely helpful to me in refining and improving the format. Several people mentioned after the first seminar, for example, that there were not enough "restroom breaks." Another criticism in the early seminars was that the content was too heavy and too much for the time allowed. Accordingly I have shortened the instruction periods and expanded the small-group participation, especially the role-playing activity. We now spend twice as much time at role-playing.

The availability of the book, *Service Evangelism,* to the participants has further reduced the time required for more formal instruction. The foregoing time schedule reflects these changes and is much more feasible than the original schedule. The time goes very fast, especially on

Saturday, when the role enactments are taking place. What would otherwise be a sleepy time for most people who have been exerting that much mental effort for that long a period is a most enjoyable and fast-moving experience.

The sharing time near the end of the seminar is not only meaningful for everyone but is especially helpful for the leader, inasmuch as the participants tend to say much more than they write, and what they say is a good index of where they are.

The bench marks are an essential means of identifying those who may have special problems, or who need help, or who are simply not "with it." I have used the breaks, the lunch hour, and the time before and after each session to deal with any individual needs that arise. If someone's facial expression indicates bewilderment or disinterest, I try to sound out that person privately and tactfully.

The evaluations received from the pastors who have attended P.R.O.O.F. seminars have been most helpful. One of my general purposes in developing the P.R.O.O.F. approach was to deepen the understanding of ministers and church leaders regarding service evangelism and to improve their own skills in interpersonal witnessing. The comments of the participants would indicate that the seminars have been helpful in increasing the understanding and improving these skills for those who have attended.

A second purpose was to deepen the understanding and improve the skills of more Second Presbyterian Church members in these same areas. There is no question that many of them are more confident and competent in sharing their faith. With the ongoing training that the Ambassadors receive through their participation in the Monday night calling and reporting sessions, some have become highly effective witnesses.

My third general purpose was to offer a training model that other churches could use in equipping themselves for service evangelism. A growing number of churches are using the P.R.O.O.F. model. I have many letters from pastors expressing their enthusiasm for the model and their excitement about the results.

The ultimate success of a seminar (should I say the P.R.O.O.F. of the pudding?), however, can be measured only by what happens in the lives of the participants *after* the seminar. Some indications of a successful experience would be:

1. That the participants themselves feel more willing to share their faith, more concerned to reach out to others, more confident in their ability to articulate why they believe in God, and more committed to being involved in an evangelistic program in their own churches.

2. That the people they called upon have responded positively to their visits. At our receptions for new members, many give the Ambassadors credit for bringing them into the church and they express appreciation for the visits. Very seldom do we ever get any negative feedback, and that is how it should be in service evangelism.

3. That, as a result of the program, the participants and their churches grow spiritually, and that growth is reflected in the stewardship of their time, talent, and treasure. That has certainly been the case with the Ambassadors at Second Presbyterian Church, and reports indicate it is also true in other churches where the P.R.O.O.F. training model is being used.

You will be tired at the end of the seminar, but not too tired to want to take a quick glance at the evaluation sheets after everyone has left. You will want to study them carefully later, of course, but a rapid run-through will help to ease your curiosity, or perhaps anxiety, about the reactions of the participants to the P.R.O.O.F. experience. You will find that their comments are usually positive and always helpful.

There remains only the task of taking down all the sheets from the walls, collecting the Bibles, extra copies of the handouts, and any other materials pertaining to the seminar. After that, go home and collapse—assuming, if you are a preacher, that your sermon is ready for tomorrow!

9

Preparing the Congregation

Before any P.R.O.O.F. seminar is held, important groundwork must be laid. This is especially true where there is little interest in evangelism and perhaps even hostility on the part of some who have rejected their own false images of what evangelism is. For some people, evangelism means calling on backsliding members. For others, it means distributing pamphlets or Bibles in the neighborhood. For others, it may mean taking a religious census every now and then. But for very few does it mean the kind of outreach and involvement implicit in service evangelism. The question is, How do we pastors go about preparing a congregation to accept this kind of evangelistic responsibility?

I. SHARING THE DREAM

The understanding and cooperation of the official board is essential. This is best secured not by announcing to them an intended program, but by the mutual sharing of our convictions about the mission of the church and the nature of their ministry. Some time needs to be set apart for this purpose, perhaps on a retreat or at least at a special meeting of the board, to permit the kind of in-depth discussion that needs to take place. In the course of the discussion we shall have an opportunity to express and explain our ideas about evangelism, hoping to enlist the board's enthusiastic support of a dream we shall shape and share together, a dream of spiritual as well as numerical growth, of deeper personal faith and greater social outreach.

At the same time we shall want to begin to prepare the congregation through our preaching ministry. This affords us our greatest opportunity to lead our flock in the direction they must go if they are to be true to the Great Commission laid upon us all by the Lord Jesus Christ. Whether we are beginning a new ministry or have been in our present pastorate for a number of years, we should pave the way from the pulpit before launching any evangelistic campaign. Program must always be undergirded by preaching, especially a program about which there are so many differences of opinion, so many misconceptions, so much heat and so little light.

Even before we start thinking of appropriate sermon topics to help prepare the congregation, we should give thought to our philosophy of preaching. How do we view ourselves as preachers? What are we trying to accomplish in the pulpit, Sunday by Sunday? Does the congregation share our understanding of our preaching ministry? If we are not sure of the answers to such questions, we had best begin at that very point, regardless of how long we may have been in our present pastorate. What relationship do we want to establish between the pulpit and the pew, and how do we go about it?

II. Establishing the Ground Rules

Baseball fans know that before the start of any game the umpires meet at home plate with the managers of the opposing teams to go over the ground rules. So, too, at the start of every new preaching ministry it is a good idea to establish the ground rules for the relationship between the pulpit and the pew, spelling out what the people in the congregation have a right to expect of us as preachers and

what we expect of them as a congregation. In so doing, we
are in good company, for the apostle Paul did the same
thing with the congregations he served. There were certain "givens," certain premises that needed to be stated,
the ground rules that governed his ministry.

Like all ground rules, they had to be repeated from time
to time, and that is what Paul was doing in his letter to the
church at Corinth. When he said, "This is how one should
regard us, as servants of Christ and stewards of the mysteries of God," he was restating the ground rules (I Cor. 4:1).
He was speaking not just for himself, but for Apollos and
Peter and all his companions—in fact, for every Christian
minister ever since. Paul had other ground rules, to be
sure, but his words to the Corinthians should be the basic
ground rule for our ministry.

Our people should regard us first and foremost as servants of Christ. To be a servant of Christ is to know, first
of all, that we are *called* to be ministers, called by God. At
the beginning of his letter, Paul addressed the Corinthians
as one "called by the will of God to be an apostle of Christ
Jesus" (I Cor. 1:1). So, too, in his letter to the Romans, he
referred to himself as "a servant of Jesus Christ, called to
be an apostle" (Rom. 1:1).

To be a servant of Christ means knowing, secondly, that
he and no one else is the Lord of our life. Paul took his
marching orders from Jesus Christ, and because he did, he
was nobody's slave. He was a free man in Christ, free to
think and speak and act to please God rather than man. He
knew he would be judged ultimately not by the courts of
public opinion, but by God. "With me it is a very small
thing," he told the Corinthians, "that I should be judged
by you or by any human court. I do not even judge myself.
. . . It is the Lord who judges me" (I Cor. 4:3–4). Those who
are called to be servants of Christ are called to that kind
of freedom.

Yet to be a servant of Christ also means knowing that we
serve Christ by serving others. Paul was nobody's slave,

yet for Christ's sake he said, "I have made myself a slave
to all" (I Cor. 9:19). This is not to say that he became
everyone's lackey, to be owned and ordered about at their
pleasure. He served them not because he had to, but because he wanted to, for Christ's sake. He gladly poured
himself out for them, striving to be all things to all people
in order that he might win them by every possible means.

To feel called of God is not to think we have what it
takes to be a minister. On the contrary, it is just the opposite. We feel more like saying, "What in the world is a
character like me doing in a place like this?" But God
chooses the most unlikely characters to accomplish his
purposes in the world, and if Paul felt unfit to be called an
apostle, how much more do we! Paul called himself the
very least of the saints, the chief of sinners, yet as he
himself put it, "I was made a minister according to the gift
of God's grace" (Eph. 3:7).

According to Paul's ground rule, then, this is how our
people should regard us, as servants of Christ, who are
called by God not because of our saintly qualifications, but
because God in his mercy has seen fit to use the likes of us.
They will discover soon enough that we are human, too.
We should never let the elevation of the pulpit be anything else than a means of improving visibility and communication.

At the same time, the people need to remember that as
a servant of Christ we owe our first allegiance to him. We
serve them best by putting him first. The temptation for
every preacher is always to be popular instead of prophetic, to please the church instead of the church's Lord.

If we are truly preaching the gospel, we are bound to
step on a few toes once in a while. When we are wrestling
with the stern demands of Christ, disagreement is inevitable. But Christians should be able to disagree in love.
Christ is much more interested in our attitudes than in our
opinions. If we truly love one another, then we should be
open to one another, in our common search for truth.

One of my own ground rules may be stated as follows: If you disagree with something I say in the pulpit, you are welcome to challenge me, and I promise that if your reasons for believing what you believe are better than my reasons for believing what I believe, I will change my point of view or modify my position accordingly. All I ask is that you be willing to do the same. A good relationship between the pulpit and the pew calls for that kind of reciprocal open-mindedness.

There will be times, obviously, when persons will agree to disagree, recognizing that the final authority must always be the Holy Spirit speaking through the Scriptures. We preachers must speak what we are moved to speak by the Holy Spirit, and we cannot dare to interpret the word of God unless and until we have done our homework. We cannot guarantee that our sermons will be liked, but we owe it to our people that our message be well prepared, Biblically based, and theologically sound. We want our people to know that everything we say from the pulpit is spoken out of love and in the earnest hope that we can all learn, as Paul says, "to live according to scripture" (I Cor. 4:6).

That is what it means to be a servant of Christ. But we are also to be regarded as "stewards of the mysteries of God." The word for "steward" is used in the New Testament to refer to the manager or administrator of an estate, in this case "the mysteries of God." Here the ground rule calls for a special qualification on the part of those called to be stewards. "It is required of stewards," says Paul, "that they be found trustworthy" (I Cor. 4:2). No man or woman would want to entrust an estate to the management of someone who is not trustworthy. And neither would God.

It takes a while to know whether or not someone is trustworthy. Time alone will tell whether we are worthy to be trusted as stewards of the mysteries of God, and God himself will be the judge. To be faithful in fulfilling that role we must preach, as Paul told the Ephesians, "the unsearchable riches of Christ," unsearchable in the sense that they are too vast and limitless ever to be fully explored, too precious ever to be adequately measured. It is another way of speaking of the mysteries of God, which defy our human efforts to grasp their full significance.

But to the best of our ability we must try. We cannot hope ever to succeed if we do not know the God we preach about. How can I talk about him if I never talk to him? How can I challenge others to accept Christ as the Lord of their lives, if he is not the Lord of my life? How can I convince them that the Bible is God's word to them, if it is not God's word to me?

The riches of Christ are indeed unsearchable, and to understand the mysteries of God is an endless quest. The gospel is a many-faceted thing, and the applications are infinite. We cannot tell it all in a sermon, or a year of sermons, or a lifetime of sermons. But communication is a two-way process. What good is our preaching, if our people are not there to hear it? What effect has our stewardship of the mysteries of God, if our people are not faithful stewards too? Part of their stewardship is the discipline of worship. The gospel is like a mammoth jigsaw puzzle with an endless number of pieces. The more one comes to church, the more pieces of the puzzle one will have, and the clearer the picture will be, the big picture. The ground rules must include our people's responsibility to be faithful worshipers.

Concerning our stewardship of the gospel, there is one theme that should underlie everything we say from the pulpit, one question that defines the purpose of our preaching and teaching ministry: What does it mean to be Christ's man or Christ's woman in the world today? That is *the* stewardship question, and we hope that with God's help we and our people can discover the answer and apply it to our lives.

These, then, are the ground rules for our preaching

ministry. This is how one should regard us: as servants of
Christ and stewards of the mysteries of God.

III. PLANNING THE PREACHING

Having established the ground rules, which certainly
bear repeating and augmenting from time to time, we
need to convey to the congregation our basic beliefs about
God, about Christ, about the church, and about the Christian life, before tackling any controversial issues. It is better to test the water before jumping into it. Most of us have
learned the hard way that pulpit harangues are seldom
effective. We want to turn people on, not off. We want
them to tune in, not out. We can accomplish much more
if we have established a climate of acceptance and trust,
one in which we can speak the truth in love without
becoming the enemy.

I believe in winning the right to be heard. Our call to
preach gives us the right to speak, but the right to be
heard must be won. It is a matter of gaining the trust of
our people. They need to know who we are and where we
are "coming from." They ought to know *that* we believe
in God and *why* we believe, before they know *what* we
believe about everything else.

Preaching, then, should be a faith-sharing experience.
We attest to the authority of the word by the validity of
our own experience, which both confirms and fortifies our
faith assumptions. Our purpose is to challenge our people
to accept Jesus Christ as their Savior and to follow him as
their Lord. The underlying aim of our preaching must
always be for personal commitment, upon which the
claims of discipleship can then be laid, whether in terms
of the spiritual disciplines or Christian outreach, or community involvement, or social action. A church cannot be
led to exercise its corporate witness in the world unless
and until its people are constrained to do so by the love of
Christ.

The goal of our preaching, as of our total ministry, is to foster the spiritual growth of our people, both individually and collectively, and to challenge, motivate, and equip them to be Christ's men and women wherever they are and whatever they do. The emphasis is always on personal commitment. We have to help our people to understand that Christian faith is trusting in and being faithful to Jesus Christ. Christianity is a personal relationship with the living Christ, who is both the source and the object of our faith. We can try a sermon on the woman of Samaria, from whose encounter with Jesus we can illustrate the personal nature of the Christian faith.

This could be followed by an expository sermon on the man blind from birth (John 9) to stress the importance and validity of personal experience. People need to learn that they do not have to be theologians to believe in God. They can talk with authority on their own experience. That applies to the person in the pulpit as well as the people in the pews.

Along with sermons emphasizing personal commitment, there should be periodic sermons dealing with various aspects of the doctrine of faith—its meaning, its nature, its source, its purpose, its object, its rewards, its risks, its ups and downs. For those people in the congregation who are potential P.R.O.O.F. participants, the greater their understanding of faith, the more they will benefit from the seminar.

Certainly there should be a series on the church, perhaps six sermons covering the who, what, why, when, where, and how of the servant church. When people understand the nature and mission of the church and their responsibilities as members, they will be more interested in wanting others to belong to it.

Farther down the road we will want to make the case for service evangelism, beginning with the Biblical imperative and continuing with the need for, the challenges to, and the benefits of evangelism in the world today. Then

there might well follow a "how to" sermon on the art of
listening, which is essential to the evangelistic approach
called for in the P.R.O.O.F. model, followed by another
sermon on "How to Witness," spelling out what it means
to be an ambassador for Christ.

The relationship of evangelism to social action and the
church's role in society should be clearly defined and
strongly emphasized, with illustrations to show people
what they as individuals and as a congregation can do in
a community. This theme can be underscored by display-
ing on a bulletin board newspaper and magazine clippings
featuring the various service activities of church members. In trying to motivate and mobilize a congregation for
outreach and service, we find it is better to compliment
them for what they have done and can do than to make
them feel guilty for what they are not doing.

We should not make the mistake of thinking that when
we have said it once, we never need say it again. A sermon
is not like the water softener that advertises, "Once you
have plugged it in, you need never touch it again!" Not
everyone is there on a given Sunday, and those who are
there may not get the message the first time, or the second
time, or the third time, or ever. Others may get it and
forget it. That is the nature of this unique form of communication we call "preaching," and because it is that way,
we need to repeat the message over and over again, in
different contexts, of course, and with different illustrations and applications and emphases, like the theme and
variations of a musical composition. If repetition is the soul
of advertising, then it must be important for preaching
too.

The weather can change abruptly, but the climate of a
congregation does not change overnight. Careful and consistent cultivation from the pulpit is needed to prepare the
congregational soil for the seeds of evangelism. If the gospel is faithfully and effectively preached, the spiritual tem-

perature of the church will rise, and with it a thirst on the
part of some for a deeper level of discipleship.

IV. IDENTIFYING THE P.R.O.O.F. PROSPECTS

As pastors we should have a feel for where our people
are spiritually, and be alert for signs of individual growth.
We can usually tell when a person is spiritually alive and
responsive to the gospel, or when someone is moved by
the Holy Spirit to give himself or herself more fully to
Christ in service, or study, or prayer, or fellowship.
Long before I ever scheduled the first P.R.O.O.F. seminar at Second Presbyterian Church I had been keeping a
list of names of those whom I wanted to invite. I was
looking for a certain type: people who were positive and
enthusiastic about the church, sensitive and compassion-
ate toward others, open and receptive to God. I wanted
people who were seeking answers, not those who thought
they had all the answers, people who were willing to learn,
not those who had nothing to learn, people who wanted
to think, not those whose minds were already made up. It
was not at all difficult to develop such a list. Most of the
names came from my contacts with the people in various
pastoral situations, as well as from my observing them in
different roles in the church and in the community.

When the time seemed right, I began issuing personal
invitations, starting with those who I thought would be
most likely to respond. The invitations were by telephone
or in person, as I wanted to be able to explain the nature
and purpose of the seminar and answer any questions they
might have. The response was completely favorable, although many could not accept the invitation because of
other commitments. That made them automatically the
top prospects for the next P.R.O.O.F. seminar.

It should be stressed that no general invitations were
given. There were no pulpit announcements, no notices in
the church bulletins, no congregational mailings. The par-

ticipants were handpicked, and I counted on their spreading the word to others. That is exactly what happened. People began asking to be included in the next P.R.O.O.F. seminar. Before long, there was a waiting list, and it continued to grow as the word spread.

The P.R.O.O.F. "graduates" became the leaven in the church lump, and their enthusiasm was infectious. Many, though by no means all, went on to become Ambassadors, and the results of their labors were soon evident to all, as more and more calls were made on peripheral and prospective church members, and people with many different needs. The personal endorsements of the P.R.O.O.F. participants plus the work of the Ambassadors had the cumulative effect of accelerating the process of acceptance by the congregation as a whole, without anyone's feeling that something had been jammed down their throats.

V. Developing the Support System

Before we begin training people to be Ambassadors for Christ we should make sure that there is an adequate support system to undergird the calling program and to follow through in whatever ways are needed. We must be prepared for an instant increase in our own pastoral load, as the Ambassadors refer people to us for counseling of all kinds. More and more pastoral time will have to be given to the unchurched in our community.

For that reason it is imperative that the deacons, elders, and other members of the church be alerted and equipped to participate with us in that ministry. In the Oak Lane Church the deacons, whose one main function had been to conduct the Every Member Canvass, soon discovered the true nature of their ministry of compassion, which extended far beyond the walls of their own church. "They acquired hospital beds, wheelchairs, and other equipment and made them available to families who could not afford them otherwise. They helped find suitable retirement homes for the aged and infirm with no one to care for them, visited the sick and lonely, provided emergency food and clothing for the indigent, sought jobs for the unemployed, tape-recorded the worship services for shut-ins, provided transportation to church for anyone who needed it, and ministered in many other useful ways to all kinds of people in all kinds of circumstances." (*The Oak Lane Story,* p. 26.)

At Second Presbyterian Church we have established what is termed the ministry of the church-in-community, with a member of our ministerial staff serving as the coordinator, whose role, in a word, is to mobilize the resources of the church to serve the community. That translates into a rather detailed description of an exciting ministry of outreach, which parallels and dovetails with our evangelism program and with the work of the deacons. Welfare cases, for example, may be referred to the Deacons Benefactions Committee or the Human Resources Committee, while community needs, area problems, and conditions affecting groups and classes of people are dealt with by the Church-in-Community Committee.

An example of the latter type is our Children's Health Clinic, which provides weekly care for well and sick children for a housing development of disadvantaged families in our parish area. The free medical clinic is operated by volunteer medical and health care professionals from Second Presbyterian Church with the sanction of the Marion County Health and Hospital Corporation. The doctors, dentists, nurses, and others who give their time in this way see their involvement as part of their Christian service to the community. (See Appendix F for a complete description of the Church-in-Community ministry of Second Presbyterian Church.)

The members of the session, church council, or whatever you call the official board responsible for examining and receiving new members, will have to be prepared for the extra meetings required to receive the people who respond to your evangelistic outreach. Candidates for church office should be informed of and agree to accept their responsibilities in this regard before they are nominated. Some training will be needed to equip the elders or the board members for this important duty (see Chapter 4).

Later on you will be able to use volunteers to help in the office preparing the calling lists, summary reports, and records of calls; to provide refreshments for the callers and to help in the kitchen; to help recruit callers each week; to baby-sit for the children of couples who wish to take part and for parents who want to attend the inquirers classes; and to help in various other ways that will become apparent from time to time.

The congregation as a whole is very much a part of the support system. As people begin to respond to the calls of the Ambassadors, the number of visitors on Sunday morning will increase. Your members should be reminded often of the importance of greeting strangers warmly and making them feel welcome. The friendliness of the congregation will do much to create a favorable first impression. We pastors can help our flocks to "think friendly."

It goes without saying that the whole enterprise must be supported constantly with prayer, beginning with a petition for the Holy Spirit to raise up people for the P.R.O.O.F. seminars, and for some to be inspired to serve as Ambassadors. Once the calling program gets under way both the Ambassadors and the people upon whom they call should be a regular concern of the intercessory prayer circles.

10

After P.R.O.O.F., What?

The real challenge of an evangelism program in the local church is not to get started but to keep going! I have heard too many pastors say, "Oh, we did that sort of thing several years ago." The question is, Why aren't they doing it now?

A P.R.O.O.F. seminar is a valuable experience for those who attend, if only as a spur to their spiritual development. But it is also intended to produce some new callers for the church, men and women who have been motivated and equipped to serve as ambassadors for Christ. So the next question is, After P.R.O.O.F., what?

I. The Calling Program

It is hoped that a number of the seminar participants will have committed themselves to participate in the calling program the following week. I don't believe in twisting arms, but I do ask the class at the close of the seminar if each person would be willing to set aside at least one night a month to make calls for the church. I assure them that their calls will be no more and probably less difficult than their role-playing enactments, that they will be teamed with an experienced lead caller, and that they will undoubtedly enjoy the experience.

"Operation Doorbell" in the Oak Lane Church was gov-

erned by three essential principles which the experience
of twenty years has verified for me. Any visitation evangelism training program must be: consistent or it won't be
sustained, top priority or it won't be supported, and well
organized or it won't be effective.

A. Scheduling

To be consistent you must set aside a regular time for
calling. If it is hit or miss, it won't last. So the first thing for
you and your committee to decide is when the calling is
going to take place. No matter what night or day of the
week you choose, it will not be convenient for some people. At Second Presbyterian Church we chose Monday
night because it appeared to be the least busy night for
most people, and we have found that our "contact percentage" has been amazingly high. It is imperative to establish a definite schedule and stick to it. There are always
those persons who want you to give them some cards and
let them pick their own time to make their calls. Don't
ever give in to that suggestion! At best it creates more
work for the coordinator, makes it much harder to keep
track of the cards, and eliminates the opportunity for the
callers to share the results of their calls and to learn from
one another in the process. At worst it invites duplication
or delay, frustrates the follow-up process, and leads to
confusion if not chaos. I repeat: schedule a definite day and
time and build it into the weekly church calendar.

Over the years I have advocated scheduling the calling
on a roughly three-months-on and three-months-off basis.
The actual calling period may extend two or three weeks
longer, depending largely on the weather. In Indianapolis
as in other cities with similar climates, it is undoubtedly
better to call during fall and spring, as inclement winter
weather and summer vacations make the latter seasons
less productive for calling. The pastor and certain others
may continue to make calls during the "off" months, of
course, while the formal visitation program is in recess.

But you will find that the ambassadors will return to their work with renewed vim and vigor, after a respite of two or three months.

Evangelism is not likely to be a top priority in the church if it is not a top priority with the pastor. It has to be something mighty unusual and important to make me miss a calling night. I want the congregation, as well as the Ambassadors, to know how important I consider this work to be. The best way I can demonstrate that is to be there with them, sharing their experiences, answering their questions, encouraging their labors Monday night after Monday night. And what a golden opportunity for me to teach the Ambassadors, whose ongoing training I have made my personal responsibility. I suggest you do the same!

B. Ambassador Groups

Larger congregations may want to consider a plan that we have implemented with some success at Second Presbyterian Church. In lieu of having all of the Ambassadors meet at one time and place each week, we have organized them into small groups who have agreed among themselves to meet on a mutually convenient day to make their calls and share the results with one another. This is not a departure from the principle of a definite schedule but rather a modification of its application, to help cope with the inevitable "dropout" problem. Each of the small groups would have its own regularly scheduled meeting time, and would follow the same format as all the other groups.

Such a program requires that there be a qualified leader in each group who is responsible for picking up the calling assignments each week, distributing the cards to the members of the group, receiving them after the calls are made, and returning them to the church office. A volunteer coordinator, church secretary, or even the pastor has to sort and file the cards and make appropriate referrals when follow-through is required. The Ambassador Group leader is also responsible for "chairing the sharing," and should be an experienced Ambassador who can facilitate the learning process for the individuals in the group.

I am convinced that a small-group ministry is essential to the spiritual growth of any large congregation. We are using a modified version of the Yokefellow plan at Second Presbyterian Church, which allows for several different types of group. Some are primarily prayer groups, some are mission-oriented, some are Christian literature groups, some are strictly Bible study, and some are primarily for fellowship. But there is fellowship and sharing in all of them, and the underlying purpose is to enable the people involved to build Christian friendships and help óne another to grow spiritually. The Ambassador Groups are part of that ministry, their program being centered on their calling and the sharing that takes place afterward.

C. The Format

Some pastors prefer to have the callers meet at the church for briefing and assignments, while others would rather meet in various homes. We have tried it both ways, and there are advantages to each. On the one hand, it is good for people to have an opportunity to be in one another's homes, and a cozy family room provides a pleasant atmosphere for fellowship when the teams gather to report on their calls. On the other hand, some living rooms may not be big enough to accommodate all the callers comfortably, whereas there is always enough space to meet at the church, should there be a large turnout. Also, everyone knows where the church is.

In either case the callers are supposed to be at the appointed place at seven fifteen in the evening. As they arrive they are teamed with their partner for that night, given a packet of cards representing homes in the same area of the city, and a map to help them locate the addresses. After any necessary instructions have been given, and a closing prayer has been offered, the callers depart, by seven thirty if possible, equipped with copies of the church bulletin and the latest issue of the church newsletter. They are not supposed to ring any new doorbells after nine o'clock, which rule gets them back to the meeting place at a reasonable hour.

Since all the Ambassadors have attended a P.R.O.O.F. seminar, they know what is expected of them in service evangelism. Even so, newcomers may feel more comfortable being teamed with an experienced caller, who will take the lead on the first night. We mix the teams from week to week, so that people have an opportunity to call with different partners. We hope that there will be an even distribution of the sexes, so that every woman can have a male escort. A team of two women is permissible, if it is agreeable with them, but I would never ask a woman to go by herself at night. Nor do I recommend calling teams of more than two persons. To give an evangelistic callers' version of a familiar cliché, "Two's company, three's a committee!" Ambassadors are there to relate, not to intimidate.

Either the pastor or the evangelism chairperson should be responsible for appointing the teams and giving them their calling assignments. The calls made by the Ambassadors at Second Presbyterian Church fall into three main categories: "probe" calls, for which we have had no previous contact or information; "follow-through" calls on homes where there has been a previous contact; pastoral calls on our own members.

In making a probe call the Ambassadors may have nothing more than the resident's name, obtained from a *criss-cross telephone directory,* which lists the telephone numbers and names block by block, rather than alphabetically. Every city and suburban church should own one. Often the callers will not have the name of the resident, as they ring a doorbell. Their agenda is to extend the greetings of the church to its neighbors, to offer a helping hand if needed, to share their faith if invited to, in the style described in Chapter 6. Failing all else, they should at least try to discover the family's religious affiliation.

If the probe call reveals a family to be unchurched or if it appears that our church can be of help in some way, the card is marked for a follow-through call, to be made as suggested by the probe callers and indicated on the card. The record-keeping system will be described in fuller detail later. For now I simply want to point out that the second major category of calls can represent as many different kinds of need as there are cards! The only thing the cards have in common is that they all indicate that a previous contact has been made and the family or individual is unchurched or in need of some kind of assistance which our church can provide. That assistance may be merely a matter of referring the people to some agency that can offer the kind of help needed, or to a church of their particular persuasion if that is what they are looking for. "Unchurched" is defined as "having no local church affiliation." Unchurched persons are listed as prospective members, and their cards remain in our active follow-through file until they move out of our community, join a church, or die.

We have hundreds of cards in our active file, which must be continually "thumbed through and mulled over" by the person responsible for making the calling assignments. That person has to study the comments to see which cards should be pulled for follow-through calls each week. The Holy Spirit is very much a part of this process, as time and again the callers report that a particular visit came just at the right time.

The pastoral category includes calls on backsliding members or persons with special needs, such as shut-ins and semi-invalids. The latter are only a secondary responsibility of the Ambassadors, who are assigned such calls from time to time as an extension of the deacons' ministry of compassion. Most of the Ambassadors are capable of handling calls in any of the three categories, but some have discovered after a period of time that they are more comfortable with a particular type of call, be it a probe call or a call on a backslider. We try to take such preferences into account in making the assignments.

I prefer that husbands and wives do not call together initially in order to prevent their becoming locked into established patterns of behavior in which one has traditionally been the more dominant and aggressive partner. Assigning them to different partners the first two or three weeks enables them to develop their individuality as callers. Later they can be teamed with their spouse, with instructions to alternate taking the lead. In the long run it is better for husbands and wives to call together, as they can share their experiences and their continued concern for the families they have visited. The work of the Ambassadors is one church activity which spouses can enjoy together, and in which they can serve and grow together spiritually.

The cards are grouped geographically in packets of five or six, with the "most urgent" cards on the top of the stack. The callers know they are to go to those homes first. Ambassadors making probe calls should be given twice as many cards, since probe calls take less time. We use four-by-six-inch cards, with spaces for the name, address, location (i.e., how to get there), telephone number, code letter, indicating prospective membership status, and an identification number (see Appendix E-1). The rest of the card is blank so the callers can note the results of their call. Every entry must be dated and initialed by the callers, with any special instructions for follow-through clearly indicated. The caller should read the card carefully before making the call, but never refer to it while in the home. It is best to leave the card in the car, or at least keep it out of sight during the call.

There are always some cards that should be earmarked for the pastor, such as those indicating a need for counseling or some other pastoral service. Sometimes I go alone and sometimes I take an Ambassador with me, as part of his or her ongoing training. There is an excellent opportunity between calls to discuss in the car the what, why, and how of each call.

With the population as transient as it is, there are far more calls to be made than we can possibly keep up with. Our probe calls have been limited to our parish area, beginning with the homes closest to the church and moving out in an ever-widening circle until the radius is about two miles. Calls on those who have signed visitor cards in church or on families referred to us by friends and neighbors cover a much wider geographical area. When you have exhausted the list of those who have already expressed interest in the church, the best way to build your membership-prospect list is to start making probe calls. The principles of service evangelism and the style of interpersonal witnessing described in the earlier chapters apply in either case.

The literature that the callers take with them will vary with the nature of their calls. If they are making follow-up calls on prospective members, they may need some pamphlets on "how to join the church," along with some informational material on the church, including the services and programs which the church has to offer. The best calling card is the church bulletin, which can be left in the mailbox with a handwritten note on it if the people are not at home. This, by the way, is another good reason for having an attractive church bulletin. Whether it is mimeographed or printed, it should be well laid out and grammatically correct. The appearance of many church bulletins can be much improved simply by changing the layout and typography. If you can't do it yourself, get someone in the church who knows about such things to help you.

The first thing the Ambassadors should do when they return from making their calls is to write their summaries on the respective cards. We hope that one of the calling partners can write legibly enough for the next callers to be able to read the entry. When all the teams have returned, you are ready for the "Afterglow," which, for the Ambassadors, is the frosting on the calling cake.

D. The "Afterglow"

I don't know who first thought of dubbing it the Afterglow, but I can't think of a better name for the reporting time following the calls. It is a sharing time and a learning experience for all concerned, as each team reports around the circle. As I have already mentioned, this is a golden teaching opportunity for the pastor, who should be constantly looking for occasions to help the callers learn from one another's experience. ("What did you do when the wife started berating her husband for not going to church?" . . . "What did you say to the unmarried couple who wondered if they would be welcome in the church?" . . . "How do the rest of you feel about the way Bill and Mary handled that situation?" . . . etc.)

As the teams arrive, the pastor or other person conducting the Afterglow should ask for the basic information needed for whatever cumulative statistics are being kept on the calling program. We are keeping a record of the number of callers participating each night, the number of doorbells rung, the number of contacts made, the number of not-at-homes, the number of new unchurched families and individuals, and a breakdown by type of call (Appendix E-2). These figures are added to the cumulative totals and reported to the Ambassadors each night. As the months go by, the totals are a more and more impressive record of the work of the Ambassadors.

In reporting the results of their calls the teams should not repeat the data they have written on their cards. Rather, they should focus on any unusual situation they may have encountered, whether positive or negative, and discuss how it went and what they learned from the experience. At this point you are more interested in the callers' reflections on their own feelings and effectiveness than in their impressions of the people they called upon. ("I think Jack did a beautiful job of drawing them out, and after they had shared so openly with us, it just felt right that we should offer to close with prayer. We were both surprised when they said they would rather we didn't. Where did we go wrong?" . . . etc.)

The temptation is to allow the reporting session to go on too long. We try to conclude before ten o'clock, to enable the callers to get home at a reasonable hour. Even so, it makes a rather long evening, when their travel time is added. Most of their calls will be within a fifteen-minute drive from the church, and normally you should be ready to begin the Afterglow between nine fifteen and nine-thirty. That allows you at least a half hour for the reports and a closing prayer. I try to stop promptly, with the understanding that if anyone wants to discuss a particular problem after the meeting, I'm available. Remind them to date, initial, and turn in their cards.

The Afterglow is a tremendously important time for the Ambassadors, because the cumulative results are always positive and the overall effect is always inspiring. When a particular team has a discouraging night, i.e., they ring five doorbells and find no one at home, their spirits are buoyed by the enthusiastic reports of their fellow Ambassadors. They soon come to know that there will be good nights and bad nights, but far more good than bad, and the overall effect is always good. They also learn that even the so-called bad nights aren't wasted, for they have left their calling cards wherever they have been, and that in itself is an important reminder that the church has been there!

The esprit de corps that develops among the Ambassadors is heartwarming indeed. There are plenty of laughs during the Afterglow, and not a few tears, as the callers share their feelings with one another. Light refreshments add to the enjoyment of the occasion. These can be provided by the host and/or hostess, if you are meeting in a private home, or by a group of volunteers who make that their contribution to the program, if you are meeting in the church. It is no burden if some of the callers stay for a few minutes to help clean up after the Afterglow!

E. On-the-Job Training

Those who attend a P.R.O.O.F. seminar do not have to become Ambassadors, but those who want to become Ambassadors have to attend a P.R.O.O.F. seminar. Such a concentrated course cannot be expected to produce callers who are immediate experts, however. The expertise comes with the on-the-job training which experience alone makes possible.

The pastor or someone who has had the training must be responsible for seeing that the calls which the Ambassadors make are a learning experience, not occasions for solidifying bad habits. Since the leader cannot accompany each team as the call is made, the only way the leader can form an impression of how the call was handled is from the Ambassadors' own report. The leader must help the Ambassadors to learn to evaluate their own calls by continually reminding them of the principles of service evangelism and interpersonal witnessing as they apply to various situations encountered week after week. The Ambassadors should also be reminded of the questions they are supposed to ask themselves after each call, and they should be encouraged to check out their self-assessments with their calling partner and with the other Ambassadors during the Afterglow. Those who consistently report that their calls have been a faith-sharing experience should be asked to tell the other callers what they have learned. Those who have been instrumental in leading people to commit their lives to Christ and the church should share how they go about it. On the other hand, those who have problems or hang-ups with any aspect of interpersonal witnessing should also be encouraged to share them. In that way everyone can learn from everyone else, and on-the-job training will take place. A study of the cards of those who eventually join the church will quickly indicate who the most effective "closers" are. If after a year of calling a person is not a more effective ambassador for Christ, the training program is not what it ought to be.

F. Record-Keeping

The discussion above presents one reason for keeping good records. There are other important reasons, such as the avoidance of duplicating calling assignments, the elimination of wasted time and energy spent in selecting cards for calling, and the availability of information on every family upon whom the Ambassadors have called.

We keep a participation record for all the Ambassadors, along with a list in numerical order of every prospective church family or individual. To facilitate the task of reviewing the cards for purposes of following through in whatever ways are indicated, it is essential to have some manner of classifying the cards, although such a system is of necessity arbitrary and certainly not infallible.

The letter C indicates that the persons do not belong to a local church, regardless of the reason. The reason could be that the persons are atheists or ones whose membership is in a church two hundred miles away.

The letter B indicates that the persons have shown definite interest in joining the church, by attending worship services occasionally or perhaps even the inquirers class, but they have not yet committed themselves to join.

The letter A is used for those who have definitely committed themselves by asking us to send for their letter of transfer or indicating that they want to join on confession or reaffirmation of faith.

Cards marked D are for people who have not yet been called upon and whose religious affiliation we do not know.

When a call has been made and the religious affiliation is determined, the card will either become a C card or will be placed in the nonprospect file, assuming that no other follow-through is required.

If a family indicates that it is looking for a different denomination, its card is given the letter E, which signifies that the family should be referred to a nearby church of that denomination. The card is kept in a separate section of the file and is not added to the prospect list. We call back on such a family after a few months to see if it has affiliated with the church to which we have referred it, or with some other church. If not, the card may be changed from E to C.

Whenever some other kind of need is discovered, the letter N is added, and these cards are earmarked for special follow-through on our part. The N remains until we have done all we can do.

These designations are for our own use only, of course, and they are constantly changing as the prospective families become more interested, or less interested, in joining the church. When hundreds of cards are involved, some kind of classification system for easy identification and quick retrieval is needed. Nonprospect cards are kept in a special file, as are the cards of those who join the church. Since the working cards are grouped in so many different categories and are constantly being shifted from one grouping to another, it is necessary to maintain a complete alphabetical master file, against which all names can be checked. This is the only way to avoid duplication and to ascertain whether or not a working card exists for a particular name. The duplicate cards in the master file are a different color from the working cards and have only the basic information, not the callers' reports. The numerical list provides a running total on the number of prospect cards, and is a useful cross-index.

I have mentioned that we also keep running totals on the number of doorbells rung, the number of contacts made, etc., which information enables us to check our contact percentage and to figure how many calls it takes to produce a given number of new members. It also enables us to project the church's growth pattern much more accurately.

The card files should always be kept in a safe place at the church, where the pastor, the evangelism chairperson, the Ambassador Coordinator, or other responsible person can have ready access to them to review the entries from time to time. When cards are distributed to the various Ambassador Groups, a careful record of the names and numbers should be kept and a prompt accounting by the group leaders maintained. It is important to know who has what cards at all times, in order to avoid having some of them lying forgotten in the purse or pocket of a caller who may absentmindedly have taken them home one night.

G. Following Through

As the number of N cards increases, you may want to enlist a volunteer to coordinate the follow-through process. That person's responsibility is to see that the proper referrals are made and that the results of the referrals are reported. The object of concern may be an elderly widow needing someone to do some errands for her, in which case the deacons would be asked to follow through. It may be a shy teen-ager wanting to become involved in a youth group, or a family needing financial assistance, or a person seeking pastoral counseling. Whatever the need, an appropriate referral will be made, and the coordinator's job is to see that the proper individual or organization follows through.

The impact on the congregation of such a program is electric. As more and more people become aware of and involved in helping to meet the needs of others, they will discover what it means to be a servant church, and the church will grow in spirit and in number. That is part of what I call the pudding of the P.R.O.O.F. approach.

II. The Pudding of the P.R.O.O.F.

By the phrase "the pudding of the P.R.O.O.F." I mean
the benefits of service evangelism. There are many, beginning with the effect of the program on the Ambassadors
themselves.

A. The Callers

The effect is reflected in the personal stewardship of the
callers, in their ability to articulate their faith, in their
increased involvement in the life and work of the church,
in their overall attitude. There is no doubt that the Ambassadors are always among the most positive and supportive
members of the church. They are its best representatives.
They have no vested interest in a particular church organization; they espouse them all!

The Ambassadors are also among the most responsive to
the preaching and teaching ministry of the church. Their
spiritual appetites have been whetted and they want to be
fed. They are the most faithful worshipers, the most loyal
workers, the most effective witnesses. They can be
counted on! If there were no other benefits to be derived
from P.R.O.O.F., the impact on the Ambassadors themselves would be dessert enough.

B. The Church

But that's not the whole pudding, for the entire church
benefits from P.R.O.O.F., as the Ambassadors become the
flavor that gives tang to the dish. Church attendance increases as more and more visitors appear in church. There
is a general feeling of excitement and joy on a Sunday
morning, as others in the congregation catch the spirit of
the Ambassadors and begin to extend a cordial welcome
to strangers. A congregation with a reputation for being
cold and stuffy is soon transformed into a warm and
friendly church.

The church school will also feel the positive effects of the influx of new people as the enrollment increases and new members become involved in the Christian education program. At the time of this writing nearly half of the 160 volunteers on the church school staff at Second Presbyterian Church had joined the church within the past four years. Our new members are involved in every activity and organization of the church.

And when it comes to financial support, they are contributing more than their share. The average annual pledge of those who have joined the church under the present orientation program is higher than the congregational average, despite the fact that many of the new members are joining on confession or reaffirmation of faith, and have not been in the habit of supporting a church. For many it has necessitated a major adjustment in their family budget.

A calling program will inevitably change the demographic profile of the congregation, as people of different economic, social, and racial backgrounds, different educational levels, different political, philosophical, and theological perspectives respond. Every inquirers class at Second Presbyterian Church includes people from a variety of nationalities and religious backgrounds. What an exciting influx for any congregation, which will no longer be a club whose members belong to the same social class, but will become what they are called to be, a fellowship of like-minded people who recognize their oneness in Christ.

A prosperous suburban church will surely lose its "country club image" as more and more of its members become involved in a ministry of outreach. It is thrilling to see the myriad ways our members are serving the community, both as individuals and as a congregation. We may not be there yet, but we have come a long way toward becoming a servant church.

C. The Community

It should not be overlooked that part of the pudding of P.R.O.O.F. is the impact of the church's ministry on the community. There is no way to measure it, of course. We see only the tip of the iceberg. We know how many calls we have made, but who knows how many seeds have been sown? We know how many people have joined our church, but who knows how many other lives have been touched? We know the names of those to whom we have ministered, but who knows how much that ministry has meant to their families and friends?

One of the amazing discoveries of those who engage in service evangelism is the friendliness of most people. In the thousands of calls our Ambassadors have made since we began the program, we can count on the fingers of one hand the number of occasions when anyone was rudely treated. As we reach out in love to others, our neighbors are almost always impressed by our genuine concern even when they are not interested in joining the church. And most do not, for whatever reason. Yet they open their doors to our callers. Be they churched or unchurched, Roman Catholic or Jewish, rich or poor, young or old, black or white, they almost always seem glad to see us. Many are not interested, but very few, if any, have been unfriendly.

What about neighboring churches? When one church engages in service evangelism, other churches also benefit. As one member of the Oak Lane Ministerium said to me, "We're glad you Presbyterians are ringing doorbells, because we've had more prospects referred to us since you started your evangelism program than we've ever had before!" That will always be true, if you bend over backward to avoid proselytizing.

Every church should have its own evangelistic outreach. I am generally not in favor of ecumenical visitation programs, because in my experience they tend to become more of a religious census, with each church relating only to those families who identify themselves with that particular denomination. What happens to those persons who have no religious affiliation? There is also the problem of differing theologies, methodologies, and styles of evangelism, for all of which reasons I would rather see each church do its own thing. So what if a family is called upon by two or three different churches? That would be all the more inducement to join one of them. It is better that the decision be which church to join, rather than whether or not to join a particular church.

The persons who eventually do join are naturally the most enthusiastic endorsers of any calling program that helped to lead them into the church. Even though many of them are fairly transient, they can and do contribute much to the fellowship of the church while they are there, and the church can do much for them. It is a good feeling to know, for example, that you have helped to bring a religiously divided family together and sent them off to their new community as a united church family.

On another level, there is also the impact that the corporate ministry of a servant church can have, as it brings its resources to bear upon the problems, issues, and needs of the community, and upon the systemic factors affecting the quality of life of its citizens. The greater a church's resources, the greater its opportunity, as well as its responsibility, to use them in the service of others.

The impact that a servant church can have on its community has been discussed more fully in Chapters 3 and 4, V. It is enough for now simply to point out that the benefits of service evangelism extend to the entire community. The pudding of P.R.O.O.F. is a rich dessert indeed!

III. REFRESHER COURSES

The principles of service evangelism are based on the understanding of faith presented in Chapter 2. That is why the P.R.O.O.F. training model begins with an in-depth look at the nature and meaning of faith, especially the why of faith. Some of the concepts are elusive, however, and need to be repeated constantly. We have to keep reminding ourselves that faith is ultimately the gift of God. We say it all the time, but do we really understand the implications of that truth—for the way we preach, the way we teach, the way we do evangelism?

Because many of the Ambassadors at Second Presbyterian Church have expressed their need for a refresher course of some kind, I am planning to schedule from time to time a mini-P.R.O.O.F. seminar to enable them to brush up on some of the cognitive material and to give them an opportunity to reexamine what they learned in the seminar from the perspective of their own experience as Ambassadors. The mini-P.R.O.O.F. seminars will be held on Saturday and will be about four or five hours in length. That should be enough time for review and discussion.

All the Ambassadors have been asking for a seminar on the basic Christian doctrines. The thinnest part of the P.R.O.O.F. format is the section entitled "What I Believe." Fifteen hours are simply not enough time to cover all there is to cover. For that reason I am also planning a seminar on "The Basics of Christianity," and this will become part of the ongoing training program for the Ambassadors and others who might like to attend.

Postscript

In these ten chapters I have presented a rationale for a particular style of evangelism and described a method of training people to do the work of an evangelist. Those who use the P.R.O.O.F. model may discover ways to improve it, and their suggestions will be most welcome. Our common goal is to help people to become more effective witnesses and faithful servants of Jesus Christ, so that they may show and share the love of God in a needy world. That is the intent of this book, and the purpose of service evangelism.

Appendixes

APPENDIX A

RECEIVING NEW MEMBERS

Second Presbyterian Church
Indianapolis, Indiana

I. Instructions for Elders
    A. Prior to the Reception
        1. Meet your candidate(s) in the Chapel foyer. There will be a list indicating those whom you are sponsoring. Introduce yourself. The candidates will have name tags.
        2. Sit with your candidate(s) in the Chapel for the opening of the meeting.
        3. Get acquainted as you are waiting for the meeting to begin.
    B. Examination of Candidates
        1. When the Session recesses shortly after convening, find a corner where you and your candidate(s) can talk without distraction.
        2. Be pleasant and friendly and put your candidate(s) at ease.
        3. Follow this outline in your interview:
            a. Use the Biographical Information form to obtain

the basic information you will need to introduce your candidates to the Session during the Service of Reception (family, occupational and educational information, hobbies, talents, interests; anything unique or unusual).

b. If they are joining by Letter of Transfer (see bulletin): "Were you actively involved in your former church?" (Get them to tell you how.)

If by Reaffirmation, "What has made you decide to become active in the church again?"

If by Confession, "Why have you decided now to confess your faith in Christ and join a church?"

c. "Why do you want to join this church?"

d. "What do you consider to be the obligations of church membership?" (It is hoped that they will mention such things as worshiping regularly; giving of time, talent, and treasure; supporting the activities and programs of the church; etc. If they don't mention these things, you remind them.)

e. "I understand you have talked about stewardship in your membership classes. Have you filled in your Time and Talent Information form and your pledge card?"

f. If yes: "You will be turning these in as you come forward tonight during the Service of Reception."

If no: "We hope our new members will present their stewardship pledge when they join, as an expression of their commitment and the sincerity of their membership vows. Do you want to talk about this, or are you ready to fill out your pledge now?"

g. "Do you have any questions about the church?"

h. "Is there any way we can be helpful to you?"

4. Share your own enthusiasm and commitment!

5. Close with a brief prayer, such as: "Father, thank you for these new friends you have brought to us, and for this opportunity to share our faith and to talk about our relationship to your church, in Jesus' name. Amen."

C. Service of Reception

1. Return to the Chapel promptly at the appointed hour.

2. Sit as far *forward* as possible.

3. When you are called upon to introduce your candidate(s), first ask them to stand. Try to take no more than a minute per person, and limit your remarks to the biographical information and previous church activities (if the candidate is coming by letter of transfer), concluding with your general impression of the candidate, such as "I was very impressed by the way Mr. Johnson expressed his faith (or his commitment to the church, or his desire to be a faithful church member, etc.)."

4. After the Service of Reception, mingle with the new members in the Parlor and introduce yourself to any whom you haven't met yet.

II. Duties of Sponsors
  A. Service of Reception
    1. Be present for the Service of Reception.
    2. Introduce yourself to your new member(s) following the service and act as their escort during the social time.
  B. Public Recognition Service
    1. If possible, accompany them to church or arrange to meet them there, and sit with them at the Public Recognition Service on Sunday morning.
    2. Escort them to the Community Room for the Fellowship Hour after the service.
    3. See that they are introduced to as many people as possible.
  C. Continuing Responsibility
    1. Those whom you sponsor are your responsibility for the next year. Keep in touch with them. If you miss seeing them in church, let them know it. Accompany them to the Annual Congregational Meeting and other church affairs you are planning to attend. Introduce them to any organization or program in which they might be interested, or see that someone else does.
    2. Be concerned for their general welfare and keep the Pastor or Minister of the Parish informed of any problems or pastoral needs.
    3. It is hoped that you and the person(s) you sponsor will become good friends.

APPENDIX B

OUTLINE OF P.R.O.O.F. SEMINAR

(Name of Church)
(Address)

P.R.O.O.F. SEMINAR
"Probing Responsibly Our Own Faith"

(Date)

I. THE PURPOSE
   The purpose of this seminar is:
       To explore the meaning of faith
       To experience the reality of faith
       To establish a method for sharing faith
   In the process we should discover:
       That we believe
       Why we believe
       What we believe
   And so become more effective Ambassadors for Christ.

II. THE PROGRAM
   A. Introduction
       1. Getting Acquainted—Who are we?
       2. Sharing Expectations—Where are we?
       3. Stating the Purpose—Why are we?
   B. The Meaning of Faith—P.R.O.O.F. TEXTS
       1. Defining Faith—What is faith?
       2. Having Faith—When is faith?
       3. Sharing Faith—How is faith?
   C. The Reality of Faith—P.R.O.O.F. TESTS
       1. Faith Established—That I believe
       2. Faith Experienced—Why I believe
       3. Faith Understood—What I believe

D. The Sharing of Faith—P.R.O.O.F. "TECHS"
1. The Meaning—Defining it
2. The Method—Describing it
3. The Manner—Doing it!
E. Wrap-up
1. Commitment
2. Continuity
3. Conclusion

III. THE PEOPLE
(Names listed)

APPENDIX C

Date _____
Day _____
Name _____   Time _____

P.R.O.O.F. SEMINAR BENCH MARK

1. If the seminar had ended Thursday night, what one word would have best described your feelings about the experience?_____

2. If the seminar had ended Friday night, what one word would have best described your feelings about the experience at that point?_____

3. Please indicate your responses on the scales below:

	Not worthwhile				Very worthwhile
Our faith probe					
	1	2	3	4	5

	Poor				Excellent
Content of the seminar					
	1	2	3	4	5

	None				Many
Discovered new insights about myself					
	1	2	3	4	5

	None				Many
Discovered new insights about others					
	1	2	3	4	5

	Not worthwhile				Very worthwhile
The overall experience so far					
	1	2	3	4	5

4. Please complete this statement: I wish we could:

APPENDIX D

Date_____   P.R.O.O.F. No._____

P.R.O.O.F. SEMINAR EVALUATION SHEET

RATING

1. On a scale of 0 to 10, how successful was the P.R.O.O.F. seminar in meeting its stated purpose? (0=not at all; 10=completely)
   "to explore the meaning of faith"   _____
   "to experience the reality of faith"   _____
   "to establish a method of sharing faith"   _____
   Overall effectiveness   _____
2. In terms of meeting your personal expectations, how many points would you give it on a 0 to 10 scale?
   (0=not at all; 10=completely)   _____
3. On a scale of 0 to 10, how helpful was this experience for you? (0=not at all; 10=very helpful)   _____
4. What was the most significant new idea, thought, or concept that you gained from the seminar?

5. What aspects of the seminar were most helpful to you?

6. How do you intend to use what you learned?

7. Do you have any suggestions for improving the seminar?

8. Any other comments? (Use back of sheet if necessary.)

Name_____   Address _____

APPENDIX E—1

AMBASSADOR CARD   /   Code _____ # _____

Name _____   Phone _____

Address _____   Zip _____

Location _____

APPENDIX E—2

CALLING RESULTS   /   DATE _____

Team No.	Callers	Doorbells Rung	Doors Answered	No Answer	Unchurched Families	Unchurched Individuals	Comments

APPENDIX F

THE MINISTRY OF THE CHURCH-IN-COMMUNITY

Second Presbyterian Church
Indianapolis, Indiana

I. *The Rationale*

As a Christian church in the Presbyterian tradition, we understand that we are called into existence by God through Jesus Christ, that we are called to mission in response to our faith in Christ, that God is the sovereign Lord of all that is, nothing being outside the orbit of his concern, and that in Christ God was reconciling all things to himself.

Our mandate is that of our Lord himself: "To preach good news to the poor, . . . to proclaim release to the captives and recovering of sight to the blind, to set at liberty those who are oppressed, to proclaim the acceptable year of the Lord" (Luke 4:18–19). The church is Christ's agent in the world and as such must be sensitive to the needs of all persons and actively seeking to be a redemptive agent in the lives of people and societies. The Ministry of the Church-in-Community is an expression and an application of the church's corporate faith and commitment. It is intended to complement, not replace or diminish, the church's ministries of preaching, teaching, and caring for its own members which nurture the congregational community, making possible ministry to the larger community.

Second Presbyterian Church has been and is involved in society. Many members are deeply involved through their positions as leaders in business and government. Many more are giving time and talent through various community agencies and programs. The church has been generous in its financial support of community programs. This new ministry is an attempt to build upon these foundations which already exist and to mobilize our resources for ministry in the community. The development of the Ministry of the Church-in-Community is a means of accepting the challenge and opportunity to be Christ's agent in the world.

II. *The Ministry*

The primary purpose of this ministry is to involve our church more deliberately and creatively in the community and to help develop a community and world with greater equality and promise for all people. Although there are necessary ministries focusing on the nurture of church members, there must also be ministries focusing on the larger community and world. A Session committee will be responsible for the development and implementation of this ministry. A staff person will be assigned to work with the committee, and to coordinate with the Deacons, so that they are aware of and involved in this ministry.

The development of the program will require careful planning and interpretation. Appropriate means will be used to discover the available resources of the congregation and to identify the needs of the community. This information will be used to make strategic choices based on the identified needs and the available resources. Once these choices are made, the programs and projects will be communicated to the Session for approval, and interpreted to the membership at large so that they realize this ministry is the responsibility of the entire congregation.

Persons will be selected as volunteers in the various programs by a screening process designed to match their special gifts with specific needs. New and creative "support group" models will be designed to provide time for continued training, spiritual growth, and sharing by those involved in particular ministries. All programs will be evaluated at least annually and continued, redesigned, or terminated on the basis of the findings.

This will be a bridge-building ministry, through which the church will be more visible in the community and community needs will be more apparent to the church. It will involve working cooperatively with other churches as well as with public and private agencies. It will necessitate the church's speaking and acting as a corporate entity as it seeks to bring a Christian perspective to other institutions, structures, and systems. As the church begins to mobilize and focus its resources in these ways, it will be more faithful to its mission by "being the good news" as well as by "speaking the good news."

III. *The Plan*

The following is an attempt to define and outline five phases in the development of the Ministry of the Church-in-Community. They represent the areas and a general chronological order of development.

A. *People Programs*

The first phase in the development of the Ministry of the Church-in-Community will consist of designing and implementing people programs, aimed at relating persons from Second Presbyterian Church with persons in the community of Indianapolis who have special kinds of needs.

We must assist our members to become aware of and sensitive to the needs and problems of the community before we can launch any full-scale programs designed to address the causes of those problems. One effective way to do this is to involve our people with those who are the victims. As people become involved in these programs they will begin to see the nature of the needs, the scope of the problems, and the complexities of any adequate solution. These programs are relatively nonthreatening and provide a fairly adequate sense of accomplishment for those who participate.

At the same time our people will become aware of the needs and problems that exist and of the programs that are already operational in our community. In essence we shall be compiling valuable data as we begin to minister to some of those needs. The more people we can get involved in collecting data and helping to identify the problems and needs on which we should focus, the broader the base of our support when we begin to take specific kinds of actions.

B. *Budget Priorities*

The second phase is the allocation of funds. It is hoped that a proportion of the financial resources of the congregation will be available to the Ministry of the Church-in-Community for programs aimed at meeting human needs. As we set priorities, it is a sound principle that money should follow people, meaning that it would be better to have members of our congregation involved in programs before we begin to fund them. People are our most valuable resource and therefore we seek to deploy them first and then allocate funds.

C. *Professional Dialogues*

The purpose of this phase is to provide an arena for our members to discuss within the context of the church and the Christian faith what is happening in their various professions. This will be especially helpful for the staff of the church. We need to know what our professional people are doing, and the kinds of moral and ethical problems they face.

There would, of course, be a vital interchange between persons of different professions as well as dialogue among those of different disciplines. Also, other people from the community could participate in these professional parleys as leaders or listeners. The first-level goal in this phase is simply to learn what is being done. The second level is to share that information as broadly as possible among people in our congregation and perhaps among the people of the larger community. The third level is to raise the moral and ethical questions about what we have learned. All of this would be done in a nonthreatening atmosphere in which no one is judged. We hope that major concerns with which the church should deal will be identified, defined, and brought to the attention of the appropriate committees.

D. *Parish Policies*

The fourth phase builds upon the previous one. It may become apparent through some of the professional dialogues that the church needs to grapple with some of the questions that have been raised. This could be done through the Church-in-Community Committee, other existing committees, or ad hoc structures that might be created. There may be some issues so important that the Session will wish to formulate policies as a guide for those who are wrestling with these issues. These statements would be intended to support persons in their particular professional roles as they are confronted with moral and ethical decisions.

E. *Parish Power*

Finally, there may be times when the church should exercise its corporate power in accordance with formulated parish policies relating to various aspects of community life, especially those institutions and systems which seem to thwart the policies and goals of Phase D.

Suggestions for Further Reading

TWO BOOKS ON FAITH

Brown, Robert McAfee. *Is Faith Obsolete?* Westminster Press, 1974.
Williamson, Clark M. *God Is Never Absent.* Bethany Press, 1977.

TWO BOOKS ON MAKING A CASE FOR GOD

Hazelton, Roger. *On Proving God.* Harper & Brothers, 1952.
Hick, John, ed. *The Existence of God.* Macmillan Co., 1964.

TWO BOOKS ON THE MEANING OF EVANGELISM

Stowe, David M. *Ecumenicity and Evangelism.* Wm. B. Eerdmans Publishing Co., 1970.
Webster, Douglas. *What Is Evangelism?* London: Highway Press, 1961.

TWO BOOKS ON THE THEOLOGY OF EVANGELISM

Autrey, C. *The Theology of Evangelism.* Broadman Press, 1966.
DeJong, Pieter. *Evangelism and Contemporary Theology.* Tidings, 1967.

Two Books on the Practice of Evangelism

Sweazey, George E. *The Church as Evangelist.* Harper & Row, Publishers, 1978.

Woodson, L. H. *Evangelism for Today's Church.* Zondervan Publishing House, 1973.